Issues in Evaluation and Accountability

WITHDRAWN

edited by *Colin Lacey*
and
Denis Lawton

METHUEN

LONDON and NEW YORK

First published in 1981 by
Methuen & Co. Ltd
11 New Fetter Lane, London EC4P 4EE

Published in the USA by
Methuen & Co.
in association with Methuen, Inc.
733 Third Avenue, New York, NY 10017

Typeset by Inforum Ltd, Portsmouth
Printed in Great Britain by
Richard Clay (The Chaucer Press) Ltd
Bungay, Suffolk

British Library Cataloguing in Publication Data
Issues in evaluation and accountability.
   1. Grading and marking (Students) – Congresses.
   I. Lacey, Colin   II. Lawton, Denis
   371.2'6   LB3051

ISBN 0–416–74740–X
ISBN 0–416–74750–7 Pbk

Contents

Preface

The papers published in this volume were first presented at a joint seminar, organized to bring together members of the Schools Council research team and the Department of Curriculum Studies at the University of London Institute of Education. The idea behind organizing the seminar was to enable researchers from different backgrounds and with different professional concerns to bring their current preoccupations on evaluation and accountability to a critical but constructive audience. The series ended with a day conference on the issue of accountability, and brought together people from an even wider field to discuss the Assessment of Performance Unit (APU) and its intellectual underpinnings. The development of our discussion to produce this particular focus of concerns needs a little explanation.

In the earlier sessions of the seminar there was agreement that curriculum development evaluation had come of age. It was established as a special area of study in many universities, especially in the USA, and had become an essential part of any new curriculum development that carried conviction. On the other hand there was a need to develop sharper lines of internal criticism and links to older, established social science disciplines if methodology and theory were to continue to grow and studies were to improve their rigour.

A major period of curriculum renewal was now coming to an end and, in Britain, new developments were likely to depend on closer links with local education authorities and schools. The new climate of economic stringency and heightened concern about schools was already bringing to members of the group opportunities to use their skills and experience in evaluation in new areas of education. Accountability – the concern that schools should be more accountable to the community – therefore grew as an area of discussion out of the experience of members of the group. The shift from curriculum development to accountability could so easily lead to a jettisoning of a valuable and relevant experience, and to a costly cycle of remaking mistakes and rediscovering the wheel. This lack of ability to learn from experience has often been a feature of new educational developments.

The decision to concentrate our attention on the Assessment of Performance Unit (APU), the major plank in the government's accountability effect was, therefore, a fairly obvious one. Although most people in the group were satisfied that the development of the APU was proceeding in a more open and consultative way than had at first been feared, major doubts persisted. There were technical reasons why the Rasch model and item banking could be a shifting sand on which to build a national assessment system. We felt that a statistical and a philosophical critique could expose these problems. The translation of an essentially academic model into a system administered at the national level, but also developed so that local authorities and schools could use it, seemed to us to bring problems that also needed debating from the point of view of those who work in schools. One member of our group who had been most recently teaching in schools took up this perspective. Finally, Bruce Choppin presented a most telling and beautifully clear exposition of the essential thinking behind the Rasch model and its use in educational measurement.

At the end of the day we felt that we had unravelled a pattern of concerns and produced an analysis of important issues that could be shared with a wider audience. After all, the developments that we had been discussing will play a part in shaping the future education system of this country during the next decade. It seemed important for as wide an audience as possible to join the discussion.

The book is arranged in two sections, each with its own short introduction. The first section contains a selection of the papers from the seminar series and concentrates on issues relating to new developments in evaluation. However, as these papers proceed, the issue of accountability emerges: first in Smetherham's paper as a background issue, but then very strongly in Simons' final paper. This concern links the two sections, for the second section contains four papers from the day conference on the APU.

The two sections are preceded by an introduction which puts both sections in a broader context. The editors felt that discussions on education are all too frequently carried out within a narrow set of assumptions. This sometimes leads to cause and effect being discussed as if both are contained within the education system. Much of what is happening today in education is related to major events in the economic and social fabric of our society. The introduction steps back in order to bring these factors into view and discusses the broad social and economic context as well as the educational context of the curriculum development movement of the 1960s and 1970s. This development fostered evaluation and many of the concerns that are expressed in the discussion of accountability.

In keeping with our 'broad brush' approach the conclusion draws widely from the literature as well as the essays presented in this book. It presents a broad policy direction for researchers in education, and although it was not discussed within the group, it represents a view that would not be violently disagreed with by the authors of the essays presented here.

Introduction

Colin Lacey and Denis Lawton

Curriculum development, evaluation and latterly accountability are terms that describe activities that have emerged as attempts to solve some of the problems facing the education system of this country, particularly since the second world war. We have not been unique in this experience and similar developments have taken place in other advanced industrial countries. Later in this volume we will refer to some of the similarities between the UK and the USA.

It would appear that certain deep-seated problems in western capitalist societies have brought forth a range of similar developments within their education systems. However, while the generic similarity is clearly visible, differences in culture and institution structures have given rise to interesting variations on a common theme.

The English education system has many unique features including a highly devolved system of responsibilities for providing education within the 104 local education authorities. This has given rise to some peculiar difficulties in organizing and implementing change. On the other hand it has been argued that the professional and regional autonomy embedded in the English system has ensured a fuller debate and a better appreciation of the problems facing the education systems of modern countries. Certainly some of the major institutional developments of this period, for example the Schools Council, were unique and became a centre of interest for many other countries facing similar problems.

One other general point needs to be borne in mind. The deep-seated problems we have alluded to are not problems that are in the main amenable to simple or complete solutions.

The education system is the institutional means by which society reproduces the skills, values and organizational forms that are essential to its continued existence. However, in highly stratified societies (1) some jobs or statuses are clearly more highly paid and more congenial while others are boring or dirty and provide little more than a subsistence (2). Families therefore use their skills, status and sometimes economic power (3) to ensure that their children succeed within the education system in achieving those qualifications that have become essential for success in sought-after professional and managerial occupations. It follows that within the education system there is a great deal of fierce competition on an individual basis. At the same time various groups within the broader society see that they have common interests in this process and individuals combine to pursue these interests within political parties and interest groups. Some favour greater equality of opportunity while others see it as being in their interests to call for highly differentiated schools, colleges and universities. There is therefore considerable controversy and disagreement about the organizational structure of the education system. It should be noted that these two factors, individualized and collective competition, would be enough to ensure some controversy about the content of the education offered by schools (4) but there are many other causes of controversy and we will use two of them to illustrate our point.

Educational specialization has ensured that the educational specialist, the teacher, has a narrow range of skills and subject knowledge. It is unusual to find a physics teacher who can also teach biology, almost unthinkable to find an English teacher who can also teach physics. Teachers are therefore divided into groups by their subject specialisms and training. During the post-war years there has been an enormous expansion in the production of knowledge. New subjects have grown up and old subjects changed almost out of recognition. Schools have therefore also become the centre of unresolvable competitive pressures from this growth and specialization of knowledge.

The second problem concerns fundamental questions within ed_____ional theory. In particular since the second worl_____ _____se of ed_____ion has been a focus of
dis_____ f the progressive-
t_____ _ay through the
s_____ring academic
_____ time or should
_____ iding a broad
_____ imagination?
C_____ he need for the
ch_____ acquire the skills
req_____ ier interest groups
have_____ need to understand
indus_____ uraged to see its interests clo_____

This is _____ _ of the dimensions on which unresolved _____ within the education system. The fact that d__ _ements exist is not presented here as an indication of the unhealthy state of the education system. On the contrary, conflict would seem to be a necessary part of most societies (5). A better indication of the health of the system would be the *way* in which people go about understanding these differences and the *way* in which they attempt to resolve them. This book is about the methods that some people have developed in attempting to

Synthesise ?

gain a greater understanding of some of the new developments in education. By evaluating them they hope to provide a basis on which better decisions can be made in the
future. One method for resolving some of the problems of
the education system is also examined. In this case solutions that make the work of schools more accountable to
other groups in society. Clearly we can expect controversy
about whether this is good or bad. If it is beneficial then to
what people or groups of people should schools be made
more accountable and how should it be done?

If we have now established the changing and controversial nature of much of what constitutes the education
system, let us now look at the particular developments in
this country that brought about a flowering of curriculum
development in the 1960s, a concern with evaluation and a
growing concern with accountability.

The social context

Before the second world war terms like evaluation and
accountability had no special meaning within the context
of education. Even curriculum development remained a
little understood concept. The different types of school
were highly specific with respect to social class and community and changes in the curriculum came in relatively
slow piecemeal fashion.

After the war the 1944 Education Act created a new
organizational framework for much of the school system.
In addition the system of allocation of pupils was changed,
fees were no longer an easy way into state grammar
schools for pupils with wealthy parents and the 11-plus
selection examination replaced the scholarship. The new
tripartite system of grammar schools, technical schools
and secondary modern schools hardly came into being
before it was overtaken by events and new reorganization
into comprehensive schools got under way.

The dynamic for change during the three decades after the war was provided by the growth of industry and the development of large administrative and managerial bureaucracies. Manufacture and administration changed from being organized on a local or regional base to being national and international. Cheap new sources of power, in particular oil, fuelled an industrial expansion throughout the world that brought new prosperity and optimism. In Britain the expansion was far less marked than in other industrial countries but was still considerable in terms of historical precedent. The optimism about the future often took the form of linking education with material prosperity. It was sometimes argued that education produced material prosperity and sometimes that material prosperity enabled a higher level of education which in turn produced a better quality of life. This idea of a link between growing prosperity and education enabled the education service to obtain unprecedented increases in funding from governments even though evidence for any causal relation was difficult to establish. During this period the education system expanded, teacher-pupil ratios increased and the level of provision improved; education overtook defence as the major category of government expenditure.

In keeping with many periods of rapid change the effects were uneven and complex. Not all areas of the world benefited equally and here the most marked effect was the relative impoverishment of the undeveloped countries whose economies depended largely on agriculture and extractive industries. Within Britain similar uneven and complex developments took place. Traditional heavy industries like ship building, coal extraction and steel making expanded rapidly after the war to contribute to rebuilding shattered economies, but as other countries developed their own heavy industries British industries declined, at first relatively and then absolutely. At the same time automation and increases in the scale of production meant that far fewer workers were required even at the same level of production.

While old industries declined new ones developed, and new sources of employment in the tertiary sector expanded rapidly. The accompanying graph shows how rapidly employment in some sectors of industry built up while others declined.

Figure 1   Changes in size of occupational groups 1948–76 (males in Great Britain)

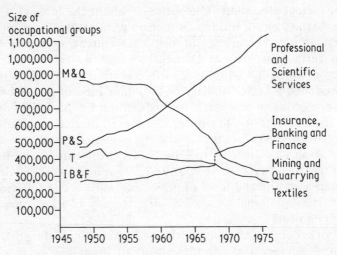

N.B. Some changes in classification have occurred over the years, e.g. in 1968, but this does not affect the general picture. Changes of this dimension have had considerable effect on education.

These trends are probably the forerunners of even more rapid change in the decade to come as these factors continue working through our society and new technological factors like the microprocessor cause rapid decline in employment in manufacturing industry and large areas of the tertiary sector, e.g. communications, banking, insurance and commerce.

The problems for British society followed fairly directly

from these major problems.

1 Many jobs in traditional industries have disappeared and with them many skills and traditional methods of entry into industry. Although schools have not been closely geared to the needs of industry, the uncertainty and the feeling of being out of touch with recent events has made it difficult for schools to prepare pupils for their first employment and enable them to make sensible choices.

2 Many new jobs have been created in the tertiary sector calling for linguistic/literary, numerical and social skills at the same time as many other occupations have been deskilled. Once again schools have found it difficult to keep up with these trends despite greater efforts put into the growing careers advisory service.

3 Regional imbalance has been caused by large losses of jobs occurring in 'traditional industrial areas' while new jobs were being created around London and in the Midlands and South East.

4 Local imbalance has occurred as city centres declined with respect to the suburbs, a problem contributed to by both the affluence (which increased emigration) and the subsequent stagnation and decline of the economy (which slowed down redevelopment and renovation). Both regional and local imbalance have given rise to overcrowding in some schools and falling rolls in others. Recent decreases in birth rate have combined with migration to produce acute problems of falling rolls in some inner city schools. Selective migration has produced concentrations of acute educational and social problems for some schools.

5 Immigration from the old colonial territories encouraged during the 1950s and 1960s because of labour shortages in some industries, has given rise to communities in inner city areas which have to overcome cultural and language barriers in order to compete with the native population. Once again inner city schools are most affected.

6   After a period of relative decline Britain's economy went into a period of absolute decline during the seventies and unemployment grew to 1½ million. Unemployment has become a permanent feature of the economy and poses a particular problem to young school leavers trying to get jobs. Once again inner city schools have been hit hardest and at a time of shrinking resources made available to education.

These societal problems are presented here, albeit in outline, because without seeing them as a context much of the educational change that occurred in this period can appear as meaningless, or worse as the machiavellian scheme of some sectional interest, for example teachers or a political party. For example, during the last five years, in particular, comprehensive schools have been accused of causing increasing violence and a depression of academic standards. Where evidence has been produced it is clear that the schools quoted are often having to deal with problems beyond their resources and certainly not of their making. Similarly, when sections of the press have analysed these problems they have often attributed them to new methods of teaching or new organizational arrangements within schools. This analysis completely overlooks the history of many of these developments. The developments have come about as teachers have come to realize that many established practices could not cope with the pedagogic problems they faced: in fact some of the established practices actually contributed to these problems.

Educational context

Three major descriptive characteristics of the education system in the three decades since the war have been growth, organizational and curriculum change and change in social function. Growth does not emerge as an obvious major feature of the system from our discussion so far. In fact, the growth of the school age group, the raising of the school leaving age, the increase in the proportion of those starting school before five and those staying at school after sixteen have led to an increase in the state-maintained school population of over 80 per cent since 1945; from about 5 million to about 9 million in 1978. Organizational and curriculum change have already been referred to and this will be examined in more detail. Change in social function has been the most difficult to observe but is in many ways the most striking. Education has moved from being a relatively minor aspect of the processes of socialization and social reproduction to being a central feature of both. Even though the unequal resources of families and class groups work through the educational system to produce corresponding inequalities in educational outcome, the educational system has become an essential intermediary in the emerging meritocratic society.

We must now examine the way in which these three factors have posed problems for the schools and teachers of this country.

Change in social function

Education has always played a role in allocating individuals to the unequal job opportunities offered by employers. During the early part of this century the type of school the pupil attended, as well as family of origin, provided the employer with the necessary background information against which to make a decision. Increasingly during the inter-war years certificates provided by the school or education system and awarded on the basis of academic performance played a role beyond their original use in the allocation of pupils to higher education. By the 1950s school examinations were of major importance in this process of allocation. As organizations lost their local base, universalistic criteria were needed to make allocation decisions. School examinations filled that role – although in many cases they were not originally intended for it. The spectacular growth in school examinations is illustrated in the accompanying graph.

Figure 2   'O' and 'A' level examination passes in all schools in England and Wales 1922–75

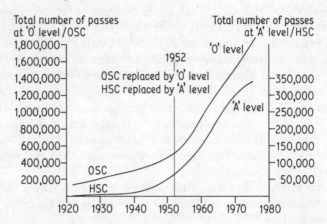

N.B. The graph is a line of best fit designed to show the enormous growth in numbers of examination passes since the 1950s. It is not an accurate representation of examination passes in each year. In keeping with Wright's (1977) treatment of this data the number of OSC passes has been multiplied by five.

The important byproduct of this growth has been that secondary schools have become the centre of a fierce competitive process to gain examination certificates. The school curriculum has become dominated by the need to achieve examination passes. For those who cannot succeed in this competition school has become an alienating and distressing experience. The growing intensity of this reaction provides many schools with insoluble problems.

Organizational and curriculum change

After Parliament and local authorities have determined the institutional framework in which education will take place the headmaster and his staff are traditionally given a free hand in organizing the school and preparing the curriculum. However, given the constraints we have already mentioned this freedom is carefully circumscribed. Schools like Risinghill and Tyndale that offend some of the hidden constraints can find themselves in severe difficulty. The result has been that schools have frequently found themselves at the centre of a set of irreconcilable demands and the subject of growing criticism as problems over which they had little or no control grew increasingly severe.

For example, the change to comprehensive schools meant that teachers who had taught in, say, grammar schools had little idea how or what to teach children previously taught in secondary modern schools. Some headmasters attempted to turn the new school into a sub-variety of the old grammar school with streamed classes (sometimes twelve or thirteen streams) and a grammar school curriculum, (albeit watered down) for even the lower streams. The high failure rate in examinations, the disillusionment and disenchantment of their pupils and the severe strain placed upon the teachers led to most schools revising these early ideas. However, moves away from the narrow examination syllabus sometimes ran quickly into other problems as parents wanted to know why their child was not on course for eight or nine GCE 'O' levels, or did not want to send their child to a school which did not have a well-established GCE stream.

Growth and contraction

Growth has emerged almost as a byproduct of some of the trends we have discussed so far. It has a number of causes, some of which are closely related to the other two characteristics already discussed.

The birthrate remained fairly buoyant after the post-war baby boom but since 1966 there has been an uninterrupted decline. This decline is now affecting secondary schools and will begin to affect higher and further education in the next three years. On the other hand children have stayed at school longer; voluntarily, to take the expanding number of certificates in education, and also because of legislation raising the school leaving age to sixteen. The expansion of education has until recently taken place at all levels and can be measured using almost any indicator.

This trend is now about to go into reverse and will bring new problems. Primary school populations are already declining. Problems of growth are speedily being overtaken by problems of contraction. These include school closures, attempting to maintain a broad curriculum as pupil numbers decline and some options do not attract sufficient pupils, e.g. second languages. In addition to contraction, education cuts will threaten the morale of staff and pupils and the quality of the service offered, and will affect the school's relation to its community.

One concomitant of the recent growth that is frequently underestimated is the growth in size and complexity of the organizations involved in education. Individual schools have increased in size and complexity bringing with them the need for new managerial and administrative skills in teachers. The trend was well established before comprehensive schools were built in large numbers in the 1960s and it became part of the thinking about designing the new schools. Some of the strains and tensions in schools are undoubtedly due to this trend. Similar developments have occurred in the local and central government administration of education.

The raising of the school leaving age (ROSLA) produced new problems for schools. Teachers were faced with teaching adolescents who in many cases resented staying on at school. They felt they had experienced all that school could offer and did not want more of it. Clearly there was a need for a more imaginative curriculum which would re-engage the interests of these pupils, or new examinations that would encourage them to work for new certificates. Schools tried both these possible solutions.

The curriculum

By the 1950s the demands of expanding industry and the relative decline of the economy gave rise to criticisms of the supply of scientists and mathematicians to industry.

Concerned university lecturers, industralists, teachers and educationalists held conferences to discuss the shortcomings of the mathematics taught in schools and in 1961 one of these conferences organized by B. Thwaites, a teacher at a public school, gave rise to a group who took it upon themselves to write a new mathematics curriculum for schools. The Schools Mathematics Project (SMP) was a national development of the traditional method of curriculum renewal. A group of influential people, drawn from high status institutions, e.g. public schools and universities, organized a reform of the curriculum within an established subject boundary. It differed from previous efforts in being able to make use of the widespread concern; the new centrality of education, the new affluence and increase in available resources for education, and the optimism expressed in the belief that education could solve major social problems. SMP was therefore able to organize on a much bigger scale than previous attempts at reforming the curriculum but it maintained a traditional structure. A group of experts, teachers and mathematicians, wrote new textbooks based on their experience, their diagnosis of the faults of the previous situation, and feedback from conferences and trials. The books were then published and were expected to change practice in schools as teachers adopted the textbooks and new ideas. The diffusion of new ideas was aided by a series of conferences and articles in journals so that a climate of optimism favouring the proposed changes was built up. This pattern of curriculum development is sometimes called the classical or centre-periphery model and characterized most early curriculum development projects. It can undoubtedly be very effective in some circumstances, and it certainly was in relation to SMP. Over 76 per cent of schools now use SMP at least in some small measure. However, the applicability of this model of curriculum development was not as widespread as was first imagined and more appropriate procedures have had to be developed in other areas of the curriculum.

Almost at the same time as school mathematics came under criticism, school science curricula were being subjected to similar critical scrutiny and found wanting. Comparisons were made with Russia and America, and our output of scientists contrasted unfavourably. The syllabus was found to be unbalanced in favour of eighteenth-century science while nineteenth- and twentieth-century developments were under-represented. Teaching methods were criticized as being removed from the way scientific discoveries were made, and therefore discouraging the very pupils that science should attempt to attract. In 1961, the Nuffield Foundation decided to fund major projects concerned with developing new curricula in physics, biology and chemistry (6).

By the early 1960s the pressures to reform other areas of the school curriculum came from many sources, and science and mathematics had set a precedent. The pressures from subjects like Geography and History were beginning to build up. In addition, the change from the tripartite system to comprehensive schooling was under way and new schools were asking questions about the relevance of the traditional subject divisions; why not combine the traditional timetable slots for History and Geography and create a more flexible, more relevant subject, Social

Studies? or should the subjects be recombined in different ways to produce Humanities? Schools were therefore under pressure from problems of internal order and organization, external pressure for more examinations and competitive success and the proposed raising of the school leaving age and curriculum reform. Many of these pressures clearly pushed schools in mutually contradictory directions. The need for exam success made the job of accommodating non-examination pupils and providing relevant (non-examination) education much more difficult.

The need to take a central initiative to bring order and resources to these problems was exploited by the Ministry of Education, and in 1962 the Curriculum Study Group was set up. The group consisted of HM Inspectors, LEA Inspectors and Organizers, specialists from Institutes of Education, teachers and administrators (The Schools Council: an official document 1971). But the CSG was regarded with considerable suspicion by teachers and teachers' unions and also by some local authorities, who saw it as an attempt by the Ministry to gain more control of the curriculum and divert new developments from the centre. The conflicting interests of those bodies, the unions, the DES and the LEAs were eventually brought together in 1964 within the Schools Council. Under its constitution the teachers' unions were to have majorities on all major committees dealing with professional issues. The exception was the committee, under the 1968 revised constitution, that dealt with finance and staff. The financing of the Council was to be shared by the DES and the LEAs on an equal basis. The staffing of the Council was to be drawn from all three areas of the education system, central administration, local administration and teaching. However, it soon became clear that of the three joint secretaries, the DES joint secretary with his or her link to the central administration and government, was *primus inter pares*.

The DES therefore retained important control by being

able to appoint to this position as well as control central finance. The unions gradually used their majorities to nominate chairmen and dominate most of the committees, and the LEAs gradually lost out. The entry of the government and public money into curriculum development, albeit indirectly, transformed the field and brought about a number of important developments which shaped the process of curriculum development in this country. The constraints and pressures on curriculum development would have been quite different had private venture capital or publishers' money been used.

The first constraint emerged from the very forces that had brought down the CSG. Many people feared the power of an organization sponsored by central government to force onto schools or teachers a centrally co-ordinated curriculum. As a result, teachers' unions insisted on safeguarding the professional autonomy of the teacher or the right of the teacher to make a professional decision about what and how to teach in the classroom.

'Its purpose is to undertake . . . research and development work in curricula, teaching methods and examinations in schools . . . to help teachers decide what to teach and how to teach it. In all its work . . . each school should have the fullest possible measure of responsibility for its own curriculum and teaching methods. . . .'

They were joined in this concern by educational publishers who feared that the Council, with its central authority, and public money, would eliminate them from the educational book market. As a result the Schools Council was to remain outside the publishing business and offer contracts to established publishers. The Council therefore lost control of an important area of activity and the detailed feedback that would have resulted from a direct contact with schools.

With hindsight both of these fears about the potential power of the Council were exaggerated. In fact the problem of getting teachers to know about the Council's work has proved to be the major problem. However, from the beginning the Council was precluded from developing an aggressive outgoing style of working.

The Council worked by sponsoring groups of college/university lecturers, seconded teachers etc. to work on curriculum projects for periods of three or more years. Most projects worked to a contract which was in fact the proposal submitted by the Director or drawn up by the Council staff and used by the Council's committees in deciding which projects to fund and which to turn down.

At its creation the Council inherited the job of furthering the work of the Nuffield Foundation (which then no longer financed curriculum development in schools) and took over the work of the Secondary School Examinations Council.

It quickly became the largest sponsor of curriculum development work in the country. To date it has sponsored about one hundred-and-sixty projects of varying size. Well-known early projects include: Geography for the Young School Leaver, the Language in Use Project, the History 13–16 Project, the Modern Languages Project (French), Project Technology, which are used in about 40 per cent of schools in England and Wales, and the Design and Craft Project, the Humanities Curriculum Project, the SC Integrated Science Project (SCISP), the Science 5–13 Project and Careers in Education and Guidance Project which are used in 30 per cent to 40 per cent of schools. Even though the use in any one school might not be very extensive the Schools Council must clearly be regarded as the major influence in facilitating change of the curriculum in the 1960s and 1970s.

The need to evaluate the projects financed by the Council sprang from a number of sources. The normal commercial criteria of sales and profits were bound to be inadequate. The Council was there to help teachers supply the 'educational needs of their pupils'. This inevitably

entailed relatively expensive projects in areas where the
return was bound to be low, for example, teaching the
deaf, other minority groups and Welsh language projects.
In addition the sales-orientated project would have been
out of step with the feeling on the major committees in
favour of professional autonomy and choice.

The bureaucratic need to report back to committees and
eventually to account for monies spent and to make new
claims gave rise to one pressure. This pressure was felt at
two levels, the level of the Council's committees where
projects needed to return for further funding and at the
level of the Council's yearly meeting with local education
authorities and the Department of Education and Science,
which determined the amount of funding for the coming
year. Much later in the 1970s, the need to account for its
research and development programme to a much more
public audience gave rise to an evaluation of the whole of
the Council's work, the Impact and Take-Up Project. In
addition projects themselves were beginning to have to
face up to problems of disseminating the results of their
development work. They needed to be able to report to
teachers just how successful their work had been in
schools.

After the early projects, project teams were no longer the
result of large scale national debates in which consensus
on purpose, and agreement on action gave rise to something resembling a national movement. Instead project
proposals frequently represented factions within subjects or
inter-disciplinary areas, and differences and hostilities ran
deep. Some of the issues touched on the deeper underlying
social dimensions of inequality and opportunity (7) and
political pressures were always involved, sometimes
clearly visible sometimes subterraneously.

During the early days of the Council the buoyant
economy and feeling of optimism gave financial and moral
support to an adventurous and expansionist policy. Geof-
frey Caston, one of the Council's most influential joint

secretaries, espoused pluralism and professionalism (8)
and saw his role as furthering the debate within education,
if necessary, funding two or more projects in a single curriculum area if important and viable alternatives were
well supported. Clearly, within this policy pressure for
evaluation also increased. The need to document the
results of these various alternatives was a logical extension of the argument about furthering debate. The Council
has become the major sponsor of curriculum development
evaluation in the country. Most of the prominent figures in
the field of evaluation today have at some time worked for
the Council or in close association within it. Despite this
considerable effort, the Council has not had a clear policy
on evaluation. Decisions to evaluate particular projects
have often been *ad hoc* and the form and purpose of the
evaluation has sometimes been unclear. This has not been
entirely the fault of the Council and its committees,
although clearly there have been times when evaluation
has been opposed by groups or factions because it was
politically embarrassing, or because it added expense to an
already expensive project.

One major problem was the unpreparedness in the 1960s
of the academic community. Universities had developed
disciplines studying various aspects of man's individual
and collective behaviour, psychology, sociology and social
anthropology, but in none of these disciplines had the
problems faced by schools featured as a legitimate area of
study. Social anthropology had been almost entirely concerned with societies with simple technologies; sociology
had concerned itself with the macro effects of education
and had only just begun to look at schools; while psychology, by far the most involved with education, suffered
from an adherence to reductionist philosophies and
methodologies. Psychologists were most concerned with
their desire to isolate and measure fundamental human
characteristics and were looking forward to being able to
harness the computer to enable them to do it. Education-

ists looking for ways to evaluate new developments in education were therefore faced with reactions ranging from indifference to an eagerness to simplify the initial problem to such an extent that it became unrecognizable. The first efforts at evaluation inevitably rested heavily on psychology, lessons learned from the more advanced American experience and the intuition and insight of often very worried researchers facing a complex situation.

Where the new developments in the curriculum were concerned with improving already existing practices and curricula, developed methodologies were readily available. Methodologies developed from controlled experimental techniques could in theory provide matched control samples so that the experimental group could be compared with a similar group that had not experienced the new development. The difference in gain scores would then provide evidence of the success or failure of the innovation. Problems with this approach emerged very rapidly. Classrooms are not like laboratories or agricultural research establishments. Education takes time and a time span of one year for a new experimental course is by no means unreasonable. During this time some of the pupils and their teachers can move into or out of the school. If the people concerned do not move then the ideas incorporated into the new course certainly do. The Hawthorne effect on teachers receiving high levels of attention from the curriculum development team is another complication. The problem of testing for effects in an area of the curriculum where there are no standardized or established tests loomed large, or if there were tests they were often tests that gave little prominence to those aspects of the curriculum that the new development was intended to improve.

These were the problems that confronted some evaluators: the fortunate few who worked with the category of curriculum development project described above. The problems that confronted evaluation of projects which were attempting to do something rather different from what had been done before were of course much greater. How could the researcher compare the achievements in one kind of mathematics with a new previously untaught variety? How could the researcher measure the accomplishment of a moral education project or a careers project? Clearly the evaluator was now in a rather different situation. There were no easy answers, no clear-cut methodologies and certainly no clearly defined group of people from whom he could accept guidance knowing that at least they were central to the decision that gave rise to the project. In fact as we have seen the groups of people closely involved with any curriculum development project were likely to have quite diverse interests and needs with respect to feedback information or written reports.

Factors affecting evaluation of curriculum development

Curriculum development at a national level and increasingly at a local level has usually involved the use of public or trust funds. The project team is therefore accountable to the sponsor for these funds and evaluation has become one way of fulfilling that obligation, both at the level of the sponsoring institution and at the level of the broader public. In addition curriculum development necessarily involves teachers in changing their teaching methods and /or curriculum to trial or develop the new ideas implicit in the new work. Clearly this can involve a considerable risk, since teachers are putting themselves and their pupils to some extent in the hands of the project team. They become dependent on materials and support and perhaps on a new examination in order to fulfil their professional obligation. The project therefore has a responsibility to teachers involved in the curriculum development and needs to take notice of the stream of information from teachers. Evaluation has become one method for gathering and processing this data. Feedback evaluation or formative evaluation is

clearly almost an integral part of curriculum development. In order to do this effectively the evaluator must
work very closely with the project team, gain their confidence and know precisely about each stage of the
development. On the other hand evaluation which relates
to the overall effect of the project or summative evaluation
is likely to be required for an outside audience. If we
remember that a curriculum development team is a small
group of people, (frequently as few as three) often on short
term contracts, working in a political as well as an educational context it is clear that this aspect of evaluation is
likely to engender some anxiety and even suspicion. David
Smetherham takes up an aspect of this problem in his
chapter.

The weakness of psychometric and quasi-experimental
methods in educational evaluation led evaluators to look
more broadly at other social sciences. In addition the early
centre-periphery models of curriculum development
which were heavily dependent on the central project team
writing the material gave way to methods involving a
more creative role for teachers who might themselves
write or propose sections of the work. This has been called
the interaction model. This changing, moving, enabling
model of curriculum development posed new problems for
evaluators. This led to the idea of illuminative evaluation,
in which appropriate methodologies were borrowed from a
broad range of social sciences, especially social anthropology. The methodologies were used to achieve a broader
understanding of the more complex process of curriculum
development or institutional innovation that was becoming the vogue in the early 1970s. The illuminative
evaluator 'takes as given the complex scene he encounters.
His chief task is to unravel it; isolate its chief features;
delineate cycles of cause and effect; comprehend relationships between beliefs and practices, and between organisa-
tional patterns and the responses of individuals' (Parlett
and Hamilton, 1976).

Norman Williams takes up the issue of borrowing from a wide range of disciplines or eclecticism in evaluation in his chapter. Following what Norman Williams considers to be an over-reaction against early psychometric techniques he gives a new emphasis to quantitative methodology.

It is of course one thing to attempt to promote borrowing from a wide spectrum of disciplines; it is another to ensure that evaluators have sufficient theoretical background and training in techniques to use them effectively. The result has sometimes been a failure to ensure rigour and effective design. Carl Parsons takes up this issue and calls for a fresh input from disciplines which have already solved many of the problems confronting evaluation. He underlines his point by calling for discipline-based research into education instead of evaluation.

Once the information has been competently gathered and analysed the issue about who should have or use the information still remains. Information can be a powerful weapon in a discussion about decisions to implement change more widely. Democratic evaluation emphasizes the right of the broader community to know about new educational progress. It also emphasizes the duty of the evaluator to explain to all those involved precisely what he is doing and to negotiate a contract with the teachers and officials with whom he is working. Confidentiality for respondents is an important undertaking in working out the final report. This illustrates one way in which evaluation has adapted to the political aspects of educational change. Helen Simons takes up this problem in her chapter and links it to the evaluation of education within schools and hence to accountability, which is the subject of the second section of this book.

Accountability

During the 1970s the economic expansion which had typified the 1960s faltered and halted. The UK's manufactured exports went into decline and we became a net importer of manufactured goods. In fifteen years our share of world trade declined from about 20 per cent to less than 10 per cent. Without the 'good fortune' of North Sea oil we would by now be experiencing an economic and perhaps social calamity. The era of optimism and expansion in which education was both an avenue for individual advancement and fulfilment and a method for solving social problems and inequalities (however erroneous this belief may have been) has almost disappeared. During the 1960s there had been persistent criticism of the major developments in education. Comprehensive schools, mixed ability grouping, the new examinations and the standards of the old, as well as progressive teaching methods and curriculum change, had come under mounting criticism from major sections of the press. It was not, however, until the 1970s that these criticisms achieved a major breakthrough and obtained a significant reaction from sections of the public. Once again it is important to realize that this critical reaction to education was common to a number of advanced industrialized countries in Europe and North America. Their education systems differ in many respects and therefore it is unlikely that any specific feature peculiar to any one system can account for this change in climate. The changing world economic climate coupled with common features of their educational systems seem to provide the framework for the answer.

In the UK the progress of comprehensivization had begun to affect the majority of school children, and the pace of educational change in curricula, school organization and examinations had been considerable and in most cases the public had not been made aware of what had happened. The competition within the education system was mounting just as the employment prospects for young people were declining. In the mid-1970s a series of events and reports came together to turn criticism into a furore which had the hallmarks of a witch hunt. In October 1975 a confidential but highly critical report on Tyndale Junior School was leaked to the press and gave rise to a massive campaign of exaggeration, false reporting and innuendo about educational standards. In the summer of 1976 a Conservative MP leaked an early draft of Willmott's CSE and GCE Comparability Study to the press and the Council stood accused of suppressing a report which demonstrated that standards were falling! Also in 1976 Neville Bennett's small study on teaching styles and pupil progress was given enormous significance by the media and held up to show that traditional teaching styles were more effective than progressive styles. By the autumn of 1976 the essentially political nature of the attack on education standards and the relevance of education to industry was recognized by the Prime Minister, Jim Callaghan. He gave ground to the critics and then promised remedial action. In calling for a public debate on education he changed the position of the education service that had developed after the 1944 Education Act and flourished in the 1960s. In retrospect it is important to notice that this period of relative freedom, innovation and growing self-confidence was a new and uncommon feature of the education system viewed historically.

The accountability movement

Seen in the way presented by Callaghan, accountability is necessarily linked with questions of standards. Accountability tends to be a question of testing. But this is a very narrow view of accountability; in a democracy accountability ought to be a two-way process rather than a matter of subordinates giving account to their superiors (see conclusion, p. 232). In the more limited sense of giving an account to a superior, accountability has had a long history in England and Wales, almost as long as state involvement in education. The first education grant was in 1833 when £20,000 was voted by Parliament to assist the existing religious bodies to fill some of the gaps in the provision of education for the 'lower orders'. But the gaps were much greater than anticipated, and the demand for money grew year by year. By 1839 a committee of the Privy Council was set up to supervise this mounting expenditure, with a secretary, Dr James Kay (later Sir James Kay-Shuttleworth) and two inspectors. Dr Kay made the payment of grants to elementary schools dependent on favourable reports from the HMI – educational accountability was born!

In the late 1850s and early 1860s there was a growing feeling among the middle classes, strongly voiced in Parliament, that money was being wasted on elementary education. The Newcastle Report (1861) suggested that teachers were spending too little time on the 'basic' subjects; the 1862 Revised Code stipulated exactly what children of each 'grade' should be able to perform in terms of reading, writing and arithmetic, and linked payment of grants to pupils' performance in this narrow range of skills – 'payment by results', the crudest form of accountability. Payment by results was disliked by teachers and also by the majority of HMI (Matthew Arnold was particularly vocal about this). They saw this kind of testing as a restriction and distortion of elementary education. Payment by results and the very narrow curriculum were gradually modified by later Codes, and by the end of the nineteenth century the system had disappeared. Elementary education was still controlled by regulations until 1926 (when the regulations were replaced by a Handbook of Suggestions); secondary school regulations remained in force from 1902 until the 1944 Education Act. Teachers were accountable to HMI and local inspectors for what was being taught and the methods used.

From the mid-1940s to the 1970s, teachers gained much more freedom. The 1944 Education Act appeared to pass responsibility for the curriculum to LEAs, governors or managers, but in practice each school devised its own curriculum. Restraints of various kinds existed, of course. In primary schools the 11-plus examination tended to encourage teachers to emphasize English and arithmetic; in secondary schools public examinations at sixteen and after (GCE 'O' level and, later, CSE) provided an evaluation and accountability yardstick of some kind. The development of comprehensive schools had two effects: primary schools in more and more LEAs were 'freed' from the pressure of the 11-plus examination, and in secondary schools doubts were expressed about the quality of education for the eleven to sixteen age group or the standards achieved by school leavers. Criticisms were often linked with dislike of such practices as 'progressive' methods and mixed ability teaching. By the 1970s this kind of public concern was reinforced by the need for cuts in government expenditure and by a desire, yet again, to see that education should give 'value for money'. All this coincided with two other kinds of pressure: first, a kind of 'consumer' movement which demanded that parents should partici- pate in education decision-making (the Taylor Report (1977) recommended that parents should be represented on governing bodies with more power); and second, there was a change in LEA management style – the Baines Report (1972) emphasized management efficiency which was often interpreted in terms of clear objectives and a concern for measuring 'output'. Almost inevitably this kind of 'effi- ciency' planning began to be applied to schools, but without adequate consideration as to whether the input-output model was the most suitable one for education.

Notes

1   It is sometimes forgotten that we live in a very highly differentiated society. Wealth is perhaps the best indicator of this stratification. The degree of differentiation is shown in the figures overleaf, derived from Atkinson and Harrison (1978). It follows that 80 per cent of the population own 15

Shares in total personal wealth, England and Wales 1972

	Top 1%	Top 5%	Top 10%	Top 20%
1972	32%	56%	70%	85%

per cent of the wealth. This distribution has remained stable for the last decade. The great majority of top wealth holders obtain their wealth by inheriting it. (See Harbury and Hitchins (1971).)

2 Townsend (1979) shows that even by the state's own strict standard some 9.1 per cent of income units were in poverty in the late seventies (4,950,000 people). But if we consider households of a man and woman and three or more children of unskilled manual status 64 per cent were in poverty.

3 If we consider ability to send one's children to public schools as closely related to economic power then we should not be surprised to find (Kalton 1966, HMSO 1968) that 92 per cent of boarders at these schools are from social class I and II while the remainder were mostly from the non-manual part of social class III. Skilled, semi and unskilled workers, sons and daughters are not represented at all in H.M.C. schools.

4 See, in particular, M. F. D. Young (1971).

5 This has been at the centre of the work of a number of sociologists and anthropologists. See in particular Gluckman (1955) and Coser (1956).

6 Nuffield 'O' level in physics, chemistry and biology were published in 1967; Nuffield 'A' level in 1972; Nuffield combined science, 1970; Nuffield secondary science, 1971; Nuffield junior science, 1967.

7 This was particularly true of the 'race pack' of the Humanities Curriculum Project and the analytical work

on race produced by the Project on Multi-Racial Education. Neither of these pieces of work were published by the Council.

8   Caston was one of the few joint secretaries to articulate a clear philosophy for the Council. See Caston (1975). Since the early 1970s contradictory pressures from the teachers' unions, the DES, the LEAs and the political party in power have made it impossible for the Council to develop a clear policy. Recent moves to develop a much closer relationship with LEAs might well enable a cleaner administrative logic to develop, while leaving the philosophical questions unresolved.

References

Atkinson, A. B. & Harrison, A. J. (1978) *Distribution of Personal Wealth in Britain*. Cambridge: CUP.

Auld, R. (1976) *William Tyndale, Junior and Infants Schools Public Inquiry*. London: ILEA.

Bennett, N. (1976) *Teaching Styles and Pupil Progress*. London: Open Books.

Caston, G. (1975) The Schools Council in context. In R. Bell & W. Prescott (eds.) *The Schools Council: A Second Look*. London: Ward Lock.

Coser, L. (1956) *The Functions of Social Conflict*. New York: Free Press.

Gluckman, M. (1955) *Custom and Conflict in Africa*. Oxford: Blackwell.

Harbury, C. D. & Hitchens, D. M. (1979) *Inheritance and Wealth Inequality in Britain*. London: Allen & Unwin.

HMSO (1968) *The Public School Commission — First Report*.

Kalton, G. (1966) *The Public Schools: A Factual Survey*. London: Longman Green & Co.

Parlett, M. & Hamilton, D. (1976) Evaluation as illumina-
tion. In D. Tawney (ed.) *Curriculum Evaluation Today:
Trends and Implications*. Schools Council Research
Studies. London: Macmillan.

Townsend, P. (1979) *Poverty in the United Kingdom*.
Harmondsworth: Penguin.

Wilmott, A. S. (1977) *C.S.E. and G.C.E. Grading Standards: The 1973 Comparability Study*. London: Macmillan Education.

Wright, N. (1977) *Progress in Education*. London: Croom
Helm.

Young, M.F.D. (1971) *Knowledge and Control*. London:
Collier-Macmillan.

Part One

1 Introduction to Part One

Colin Lacey

The first section of this book contains four papers on aspects of evaluation. We have seen how evaluation emerged as an area of special responsibility within the curriculum development movement of the 1960s and 1970s, and how curriculum development itself emerged from broad societal changes after the second world war. It is important to keep these broad contextual factors in mind. However, the essays themselves are more concerned with the necessarily detailed arguments about the status, structure and developing methodologies of evaluation. The following short accounts on each of the contributions is intended to help the reader coming fresh to this subject matter to make some of the links that are sometimes assumed by the writers.

In the conclusion we will take these arguments a step further and attempt to relate more closely the twin concerns of this book: evaluation and accountability.

A policy for educational evaluation

Carl Parsons has a background in sociology, and taught in

primary schools before undertaking research in education. He is currently working with the Schools Council funded Impact and Take-Up Project investigating the effects of the curriculum development which has been undertaken by the Council over the last fifteen years. His previous research was as part of a team at Sheffield Polytechnic examining the implementation of the Geography for the Young School Leaver Project. It was during this period that he published a critique of the so-called 'new wave' evaluation.

In this volume, Parsons takes his critique further. He claims that evaluation as a label is misleading and a misnomer for many of the activities that go on under that title. If evaluators collect and provide evidence for decision-makers, it is not the evaluators who evaluate, it is the decision-makers. The term originates from the earlier psychometric period of evaluation which is now positively embarrassing. Parsons complains that much of the research that is currently described as 'illuminative evaluation' is little more than description; some of it is even fictional. This point brings him to the major part of his critique. Current styles in evaluation do not contain enough rigour either in terms of their methodology, which takes up the point made by Norman Williams, or in terms of their theory. Established disciplines like sociology (Williams would add psychology) have already worked their way through many of the problems faced by evaluators of educational programmes and curriculum development. Not unreasonably, Parsons feels that this experience should be used and, where it is not, the inadequacies of the research should be exposed. Instead of this rigour, Parsons finds a cult of personality, and the results of evaluation research sometimes being judged on the reputation of the researchers. His final plea for policy-oriented research based on the theory and methods of established disciplines is not widely held among evaluators, but I feel that many of his concerns about rigour and methodology are growing and are having results. In their different ways, the four contributors to this section all argue for increased provision and improved design and methodology.

The weakness of Parsons's position is probably that he underestimates the importance of the pressures and culture of the teachers' world, and the political realities of the decision-makers' world. In these worlds, academic disciplines do not have much currency. In fact, for many practitioners in education, sociology and similar social science disciplines are viewed with considerable suspicion. It follows that a retreat into disciplines which have themselves become mysterious and impenetrable to outsiders might not be the best way to resolve these dilemmas. It might be important for academics from these disciplines to spend more of their time relating to the pressures of the non-university world.

The tension between discipline purity and a discipline applied to the practical world will always be with us. It is, in our view, a healthy tension that generates fruitful critiques of both positions and enlivens both. It does, however, need a minority of sociologists and psychologists to be prepared to live in the uncomfortable 'between world' relating new developments and the theory of the discipline to the praxis of the everyday world. It is uncomfortable because the person in the 'between world' can never feel completely comfortable in either. I think Carl Parsons provides us with such an argument and therefore makes a seminal contribution to an important debate.

An eclectic approach to evaluation

Norman Williams argues that since curriculum development is a complex process involving changes in many dimensions of human behaviour simultaneously, it is important to use a complex and carefully designed evaluation. Single experimental or quasi-experimental designs are seldom able to encompass the scope of most innovation. He argues against an over-reaction to the weaknesses of early psychometric evaluations which has generated a genre of evaluation based substantially on 'gut' reaction. The strengths of non-parametric statistics and the careful choice of simple indicators can be used to strengthen descriptive accounts of a process, and perhaps augment rather than replace psychometric measures, where they remain appropriate.

Norman Williams trained as a psychologist and has had a long career in education and research into education. Before joining the Schools Council as a research officer his research publications were in the fields of psychology and moral education. At the Council he has developed wide-ranging interests in curriculum development and evaluation. It is not surprising that he sees the problems with the current state of evaluation in a similar light to Parsons. However, his criticisms are not as root and branch as Parsons's, and he places much more emphasis on building on the strengths of the new styles of evaluation. The emphasis on strengthening design, methodology and statistics in evaluation are important and spring directly from his own experiences in helping to design project evaluations. Norman Williams has also been successful in introducing a computer into the Council and designing his own computer education programme so that his suggestions are based on what he knows can be achieved.

David Smetherham is a sociologist. After teaching social studies for a number of years in a comprehensive school he joined the research team of the Schools Council. It was during his work as a teacher and in his role as a research officer that he developed his deep interest in the methodological and ethical problems of participant observation, particularly when it was used as a tool for project evaluation. Smetherham believes that many of the problems of participant observation in evaluation which are dealt with on the basis of personal skills are capable of codification and study. They derive from structural strains that reoccur in projects and institutions, and it is probably the lack of systematic study that gives them an idiosyncratic appearance. While they remain uncodified and present themselves to each new evaluator as new phenomena they are bound to be seen as problems to be dealt with on a personal and *ad hoc* basis.

Smetherham therefore finds himself disagreeing with Parsons about the reasons for 'new wave' evaluators relying on personal skills, and he also doubts whether the solution to the problem rests with established disciplines unless practitioners from these disciplines are willing to explore the world of education. On the other hand, as knowledge about the process of evaluation increases, it may well be possible to improve the quality of research by being clearer about which areas are necessarily dependent on the personal skill and reputation of the researcher. Smetherham attempts an early classification of situation and methodology that he hopes will assist this process. Smetherham's conclusion brings him closer to Parsons in that he sees the development of a more systematic methodology as a welcomed additional precision in evaluation.

Process evaluation in schools

Helen Simons also trained as a psychologist but did not work as an academic psychologist before becoming a project evaluator. Her experience in schools as a teacher and evaluator led up to a university career in curriculum studies at the Institute of Education at the University of London. Her current work in pioneering self-evaluation accountability models in schools is in the forefront of research in this area and represents a different emphasis to the directions proposed by Carl Parsons and Norman Williams.

Simons's critique starts with the shortcomings of what she calls the product-efficiency models of evaluation. The emphasis in these models on what *can* be measured leads to a distorted and over-simplified view of what constitutes education. In turn, the difficulties in the tests and monitoring systems can lead to parallel deficiencies developing in the education offered to children, as teachers become aware that their responsibility ends with their children's attainment in tests. This is the lesson learned from 'payment by results'. She argues that the reliance on modern tests enables a similar if more sophisticated centralized monitoring system to be set up – this view is, of course, developed in Part Two of this book. One answer to this problem lies in developing new self-evaluation procedures 'consonant with the education practices which teachers value so highly'. Helen Simons explores how this can be done.

The problems encountered in this approach are well appreciated. One major difficulty stems from the fact that in order to portray more complex educational processes, the techniques involved are frequently also more complex and difficult. Teachers need to be highly motivated to take part in what can be an exacting and difficult exercise. In addition the difficulties go beyond technical and methodological concerns: they soon become political. They become an argument about the professional autonomy of teachers and schools, and part of the power struggle between the administrative and political centre and the practitioners at the periphery. Helen Simons does not shirk this issue and its importance for the process evaluation she advocates. Clearly if teachers reveal more about themselves in a situation of suspicion and tension due to educational cuts and teacher redundancy, they are perhaps placing important information in the hands of potential enemies. On the other hand, the process of consultation and sharing that she suggests could perhaps build openness and mutual support into a system of accountability.

2 A policy for educational evaluation*

Carl Parsons

Research under the heading of 'evaluation' has been a growth area in the last decade. 'Evaluation' may change in style and role but with its image of usefulness it could claim a larger proportion of diminishing research funds in the coming decade. Currently there is a shortage of cash and a pressing need for fullest information to make spending decisions, justify policy and 'hallmark' developments. Instead of the vague altruism of academic research, which is said to aim at 'increasing our understanding', evaluation promises ready assistance to those who make policy at any level. The term itself has a steely, pure sound about it, an awesome ring of something definitive. Its establishment as a valid field of endeavour in education is underscored by the emergence of institutions set up to promote it; the Schools Council has its 'Evaluators' Group' and in the United States there is the Center for Instructional Research and Curriculum Evaluation at Illinois and the Evaluation Center at Ohio.

I want to question the rationale for the existence of evaluators as a group set apart from social research gener-

*My thanks are due to Stephen Steadman for his comments on drafts of this chapter.

ally, and critically examine some recent trends in the field, particularly those which use the language of 'portrayal' (Stake, 1967), 'case study' (Walker, 1974) or 'illuminative evaluation' (Parlett and Hamilton, 1976).

Although what has come to be known as the 'new wave evaluation' bears the brunt of the criticism in this chapter, it should be made plain at the outset that authors in this 'movement' have done much to stimulate debate and set down challenges for established educational research. Small wonder that they have offended sensibilities in some quarters.

Evaluation as a misnomer

Numerous researchers have taken the title of 'evaluator', but while in the United States one finds evaluators in many fields of social policy (Bennett and Lumsdaine, 1975), strangely, in Great Britain it is difficult to think of researchers outside education who accept that label. It is anyway an oddly confusing label for researchers, administrators, teachers and others involved. On a mundane level we are all evaluators in most of what we do, routinely passing judgement and making decisions based on evidence at hand or that can be accumulated. Whether the issue is canned food, teaching methods or nuclear power, evidence is viewed in the context of personal values. In the grander sphere of social policy, in a collective sense, the same holds. And of course there the value context is overlaid with political considerations – pragmatism and power. Research often has to relate to these latter conditions. MacDonald (1976) is amongst those who have argued strongly for the distinction between evaluation and research and the three pages he devotes to making the case in that paper (pp. 130–3) are worth reading – and evaluating! The difficulties of handling values and in reaching relevant audiences have been ever-present in social research. And they are insufficient for the grounding of a new specialism.

I would argue that 'evaluation' is not a professional activity. It is best seen as a stage which closely precedes decision or action, which are at some remove from the efforts of those researchers who readily accept the title of evaluator. 'Evaluation' is an inaccurate term when one considers definitions such as the following: 'Curriculum evaluation is the collection and provision of evidence on the basis of which decisions can be taken about the feasibility, effectiveness and educational value of curricula' (Cooper, 1976); see also Stufflebeam *et al.* (1971, p. 40) for a very similar definition.

In fact sifting through relevant Schools Council writings and the work of many American authors, apart from the behavioural objectives curriculum developers (Bloom (1956), Tyler (1949), and Wiseman (1970)) only Scriven (1967) unashamedly sees 'evaluation' as 'judging the worth of an educational programme'. White, a philosopher and something of an outsider in this practical business, would figure as another exception (White, 1971). Most writers and professional practitioners in evaluation see the process as concerned with full description and provision of information for decision-makers. I would not argue with the purpose of such research but it is misleading and presumptuous to call it evaluation. The evaluation itself then lies with those who decide or implement policy, drawing on the findings or descriptions of researchers but setting these in the wider context of values and options.

One can applaud the trend towards less judgemental approaches to monitoring and investigating educational institutions and products but it is more helpful to see this work as little different from that of the bulk of researchers in the social sciences; the tasks are just more constrained than usual, by the demands to relate to policy in terms of topic and time-scale. The research must be *policy-oriented*. Waller in his 'Sociology of Teaching', written fifty years ago, wrote:

> If I am to help others gain any usable insight, I must
> show them the school as it really is. I must not attack the
> school, nor talk overmuch about what ought to be, but
> only about what is. (Waller, 1965, preface)

His book is relevant today and his message all the stronger
by declining to make judgements.

There are two circumstances where evaluation can be
properly applied in policy-oriented research – formative
evaluation, i.e. judgemental information feedback during
a development (Scriven, 1967), and where there are
specific criteria according to which a practice, programme
or product is to be judged. Formative evaluators work
alongside development or action research teams with the
task of feeding such teams with information that might
help them modify their work, counter weaknesses, anticipate problems and so on. The formative evaluator is an
internal critic and provides an information feedback service.

Useful as such a role might be to a project, it is doubtful
whether in curriculum development it has consistently
helped to provide answers to a number of important questions; certainly not answers robust enough to stand translation from the rarefied trial/experimental setting to the
generality of schools:

1   Is the project worth further investment?
2   Has it demonstrable contributions to make to pupil
learning?
3   In what ways is it better than what it replaces?
4   What services does it provide which were not previously available?

Few studies have shown the problem associated with use of
the project or what special conditions need to be met if the
project is to work optimally (MacDonald and Ruddock,
1971).

The formative evaluator's prime function is to inform

the project team, to which he must maximize his utility, and it can be argued that most of the information areas signified by the above questions are not his responsibility. The majority of evaluations of curriculum development being of the formative kind, information provision for decision-makers other than the project team has been seldom sought in Britain (Eraut and Collier, 1979) or the United States (Grobman, 1968). Formative evaluation has been too often assumed sufficient for summative purposes in the case of Schools Council projects and also in the Course Content Improvement projects in the United States. It is not surprising that highly esteemed and often expensive developments have in the long term been seen as having negligible or spurious effects when disseminated more widely. The distinction between formative and summative evaluation is an important one. The former serves a narrow audience, the developers, and to be effective needs to be closely allied to or an integral part of the team. The commitment thereby generated would make the formative evaluator suspect as the provider of objective summative information of significance to a wider audience. Consider three processes commonly considered part of curriculum development: design, evaluation and dissemination. These are conceptually (if not practically) distinct and not easily reconcilable; the circumstances and skills right for one process are wrong for others. This applies also to the two separate tasks of providing information for developers and serving the more extensive information needs of a wider audience.

Studies which are designed to test, according to pre-specified criteria, whether a project is successful are numerous and to these the title 'evaluation' can unequivocally be assigned. The Nuffield Primary French scheme was judged by whether pupils taught French at primary school performed better at thirteen and fifteen than those pupils who did not receive any French teaching until eleven (Burstall *et al.*, 1975). The American Headstart and Follow Through programmes were judged by comparing the gains in cognitive and affective measures of groups which had and had not experienced these programmes (Cicerelli, 1972). These studies admittedly faced big problems in their implementation. However, whether it be a formative evaluation or a criterion referenced evaluation (i.e. according to pre-set criteria), it is *an* evaluation; it does not preclude evaluation by a project team or policy-makers who will take into account other considerations besides the evidence researchers can provide. Local authorities in England responded in various ways to Burstall's unfavourable report on Primary French; for some 'it confirmed our own impressions', for others it was 'not influential' (Doe, 1976). Headstart survived a damning report, according to one American commentator, because of 'parent protests, academic pride and the fact that the social problems remained and no one could think what else to do about them' (quoted in Makins, 1978). Seemingly, even these studies with a more obvious evaluative stance are little different from those of a more descriptive, 'illuminative' nature. They are policy-oriented in providing information to those who need to maximize their knowledge in order to choose amongst policy options. The researcher might provide *an* evaluation but it still only figures as one input for decision-makers who provide the definitive evaluation.

For the most part evaluation is an inappropriate term to characterize the activity. The term can also raise problems in the conduct of enquiry. A researcher entering a school or joining a teachers' curriculum development group to study what happens, e.g. the implementation of a curriculum development project or the process of grassroots teacher developments, is more than a little hampered in his relationships with teachers by bearing the title 'evaluator'. It requires the incumbent to work much harder to allay fears and negotiate a satisfactory identity in the research setting. And it is an unnecessary difficulty when the object of the study is 'to gain a better understanding of' or 'record the experience of' rather than 'measure the achievement of'. One wonders whether Smetherham's Doris (this volume) would have encountered such problems had she borne the title 'research officer' rather than 'evaluator'.

My views have been coloured by working on the Schools Council's Impact and Take-Up Project since 1976. This enquiry, as the title implies, is providing information about the Schools Council's effect on schools and the wider education system through its projects, publications and examinations work (Steadman *et al.*, 1978, 1980). For example, data on proportions of teachers familiar with or using projects clearly lends itself to making judgements about the success or otherwise of the Schools Council. On this project we have studiously avoided the term evaluation and not passed judgement ourselves on the Schools Council but have seen our purpose as the provision of information so that others may judge, according to their own criteria.

The span of evaluation

Evaluation-type studies have been varied in empirical focus and methodology but are often judged to be of indifferent quality. Looking at the reviews of the work of evaluators in many areas, one quickly grasps the low esteem in which their work is held by academics. I doubt that things have changed much since the 1960s when one American commentator wrote: 'Although there are notable exceptions, most of what passes for evaluative research in most fields of public service, such as health, social work and education, is very poor indeed' (Suchman, 1967, p. 20). Methodologically evaluations have been claimed as suspect often because time pressures have overridden demands for rigour and reliability. Because the research is to serve social policy decision-making, restraints are imposed which have been responsible for a reluctance on the part of social scientists to undertake evaluation. Demands for 'quick and dirty evaluation' (Orlans, 1973, p. 123) make it difficult to be thoroughgoing in design, data collection and analysis.

The criticisms that are made are perhaps unduly harsh for some evaluations of merit do exist. Moreover, these appear to be principally the traditional type yielding quantitative data. Cicerelli's (1972) evaluation of Headstart received a lot of criticism, but within the caveats he makes for the report the information on the non-significant educational improvements brought about by the pre-school project is impressive and influential (Rossi and Williams, 1972). Similarly the data on 'Sesame' (Bogatz and Ball, 1973), and in this country the evaluation of the Primary French scheme (Burstall *et al.*, 1975), ITA (Warburton and Southgate, 1969) and of science teaching methods (Eggleston, 1976) have contributed widely to an appreciation of the effects of such programmes. What distinguishes these examples from studies in the field advocating non-traditional approaches is that they were associated with explicit criteria for judgement, namely 'Were pupils' attitudes or attainment levels affected by the programmes?'

Without wishing to call for a resuscitation of the earlier situation in which the psychological fraternity was ever ready with a 'You hum it, we'll measure it' attitude, measurement has a considerable role to play, and one which has found little space in evaluations of Schools Council curriculum development projects. It should not be overlooked either that it is just such evaluations which have sobered our thinking about how ineffective education is as a factor for social engineering (Jencks *et al.* (1972), Halsey (1972)). I question Simons's (this volume) exclusive emphasis on process studies but agree that measurement programmes which concentrate on product-gains in test scores are partial and unsatisfying alone. They focus on a narrow range of short-term phenomena using limited methods, thereby doing some injustice to the complexity of the lived world of those under scrutiny. The new wave evaluators have rightly sought to counter this by making the real day-to-day world of teachers the locus of their enquiries. Certainly decision-makers at all levels can be served by accounts and analyses of the effects of an educational programme in terms of what happens, how people feel and react, etc., rather than simply by abstracted reports of mean scores and variations on pupil tests.

Two recent American examples can be cited to mark the extremes in this apparent continuum from limited testing to investigations of the full reality. Stake and Easley's *Case Studies in Science Education* (1978) took eighteen months, cost thirty thousand dollars and involved some fifteen fieldworkers. It yielded eleven case study reports on science education (including mathematics and social studies) in high schools in a carefully chosen stratified sample of school districts across the country. The purpose of the report was to supply the sponsors, the National Science Foundation, with information to help it decide on how it might set about improving science education in schools (again!). The evaluation of the Follow Through programme (Anderson, 1977) was spread over nearly ten years and cost upwards of thirty million dollars. This was part of a planned variation experiment to compare disadvantaged pupils enrolled in about twenty different models of early childhood education. Matched control groups were also used. Four instruments were used as the basis for comparing the models:

1   A standardized achievement test of basic skills.
2   A test of non-verbal problem-solving ability.
3   A measure of self-esteem.
4   A measure of children's tendency to assign responsibility for their academic performance to themselves or to other people or circumstances.

Follow Through was about increasing the life chances of

disadvantaged minorities. The Federal Government needed to know which models worked best and how much impact they made; the inference accepted by both the Office of Education and the researchers was that improvements in academic performance and attitude were necessary if the underprivileged were to compete more effectively in American society.

It is somewhat artificial to compare these two studies if only because of their vast difference in cost. But both are seen as evaluations, though there is considerable licence in Stake and Easley's use of the term. It is interesting to speculate how each could have done the job of the other; Bock and associates could have examined achievement and attitude in different science programmes while Stake and his case study specialists could have given accounts of the different programmes of compensatory education. It is a whimsical conjecture but one which helps to highlight the strengths and weaknesses of each approach.

Presumably the National Science Foundation has misgivings about the quality or content of science teaching in American high schools and seeks guidance about how it may best effect improvements. The case study approach, even augmented by a survey of teachers, leaves a policy-maker short of information on what aspects of science the pupils cope with inadequately. On the other hand, whatever strategies are chosen to bring about change, they can be devised in the light of vivid, sometimes chaotic, richness of detail about the settings in which these strategies will have to work. The enormously expensive Follow Through evaluation has provoked a lot of debate culminating in a third party review of the evaluation. In this review House and his panel concluded that it was an unfair evaluation which overlooked conflicting expectations, local conditions and the variety of goals, and used inappropriate or unreliable measures (House *et al.*, 1978). The evaluators responded with a very stern defence (Anderson, 1978) under the amusing title of 'Pardon us, but what was the question again?' Each Follow Through project carried out some monitoring programme to gauge the impact of its efforts but there seems little doubt that accounts of what was happening at the sites made by qualified or prestigious outsiders would have provided more favourable evidence. The evidence would have been most apposite too, because Follow Through was conceived first as a more full-bodied effort to improve the lot of the disadvantaged through many community support and community involvement schemes – that is, before Nixon reduced the first year budget from one hundred and twenty to fifteen million dollars! And that had some very awkward repercussions for the psychometric evaluation. Although the Follow Through evaluation is partial, and the authors do not deny this, it is difficult to concur with House's disbelief at the finding that Follow Through pupils performed no better than comparison classes: 'After the enormous effort and funding put into developing Follow Through Models, this finding defies common sense . . . Can it be that so much effort had no measurable outcome?' (House et al., 1978, p. 155). The nasty thing about figures is that they can be stubbornly ungenerous with no scrap of sympathy for human endeavour. In humanistic studies there is always the opportunity to be complimentary and understanding. The strength of the measurement approach is that its values are explicit and data collection and analysis are easily made subject to public scrutiny. In ethnographic or case study approaches values need to be revealed, methodology needs to be explained and data analysis ought to be rule-governed. And this is where one questions the merit of Case Studies in Science Education. Stake and his co-workers have produced a delightful collection of readable material leavened with photographs, poetic quotes and even jokes; my first reaction was 'I wish I had been there!' But as research it is highly questionable. Stake sees this collection of field observations as an attempt 'to improve portrayal of educational programs as part of curriculum evaluation studies'. Despite the cross-checking facilitated by squads of site visitors three major questions arise about the merits of each work.

1   Values and criteria are not explicit but there is a theme of sympathy for the teachers and local administrators, their institutions, communities and history. The reports are very much from the viewpoints of inhabitants of the various locales. Stake and Easley (1978) write: 'Seeing rather than measuring was the activity of the project . . . Issues were the central foci . . . We sought vignettes and devised scenarios, representations of experience to illustrate issues' (Booklet O, p. C1). But the choice of issues seems arbitrary, selected according to impression and undisclosed values. It is difficult to be sure of what guided the 'seeing' and seeking.

2   Methods seem very loosely organized. Quite simply there is no public record of methods, cross-checking was superficial and reliability uncertain.

3   Analysis is touchingly impenetrable. Stake and Easley write:

> We debriefed ourselves *in a naturalistic way*, trying to exercise the discipline of the historian, ethnographer and archeologist, searching for confirmation and disconfirmation *in the experiences we had encountered* and preparing a report based on generalisation *drawn as much from recollection and intuition* as from formal records we kept. (Booklet O, p. C8, my emphasis)

Data or theory played no compelling part apparently. There was considerable latitude for personal as opposed to professional or rigorously justified judgement. This disconcerting suspicion is fed by Denny's report when at the outset he writes: 'It pleases me to write this story . . . My story is largely teachers' words' (Booklet 1, p. 1). Walker's introductory passage is revealed as not a factual description at all but the amalgamation of bits of information gathered at various times during the case study, welded into a coherent, but fictional, account of the start of the day for Pete, a high school teacher (Booklet 11, p. 1).

Conclusions drawn by the fieldworkers also seem *non sequiturs* to the rich description. Mary Lee Smith concludes her wide-ranging but brief study almost philosophically:

> Virtually nothing can be said about the Fall River 'Science Program' in general. The district has developed science curricula packed with articulated objectives and brimming with specified content; yet there remain differences in method, content and sense of purpose . . . This diversity and complexity, even within Fall River, suggests why national efforts to reform the curriculum become transformed, attenuated or lost entirely before they reach the classroom. The schools have lives of their own, existing as organisms exist, to be 'on with it', perpetuating themselves and protecting themselves against assault from without. (Booklet 2, p. 23)

Her first sentence raises questions while her comments on the fate of national curriculum development efforts and her view of schools as organisms are just unsubstantiated. One is particularly struck by the freedom of this case study fieldworker and the looseness of fit between account and conclusion. It contrasts with one Office of Education evaluator of Follow Through who, aghast at the unfavourable results, was reported to have said: 'I almost cried when I saw the data. I kept thinking there was an error in the analysis, or that I wasn't reading the print-out right' (Kennedy, 1977, p. 200). A similar comparison of approaches to the study of curriculum projects could be made in England. Burstall *et al.*'s (1975) results of a study of Primary French were discouraging; Jenkins's (1977) report on an Integrated Studies lesson was capricious but in an undefined way revealing. Useful things are learnt about the generality of French teaching and the idiosyncracies of Jenkins's Mr Bondine.

In carrying out a critique of what passes for evaluation I am operating with a discipline-based perspective. The biggest criticism of measurement-based studies is their narrowness but the data and canons of procedure are there to judge the validity of what they have done. At the other extreme, anthropological, ethnographic studies have almost severed ties with social science and, indeed, have quite openly moved to an investigative journalist position. There is probably a place for this but not as a replacement for policy-oriented enquiries guided by the standards, concepts and methods of established disciplines. Otherwise the question for policy-makers becomes not 'What information do we need?' but as Williams (this volume) writes 'Whose gut do we trust?'

The scope of evaluation studies has been admirably broadened and there are sound arguments for moving beyond narrow criteria for judgement. But illuminative, goal-free, transactional, responsive, holistic, humanistic, soft evaluation can still be encompassed within a framework of broad, discipline-based, policy-oriented research. Research of this sort is necessarily complex, eclectic and interdisciplinary. The full import of this has been sidestepped. Rather than addressing the conceptual and methodological implications, the attention of the evaluation community has been turned to ethical and political considerations. The movement in this direction is best highlighted by MacDonald (1976) and House (1974). Their concern about relationships with intended or potential users of their reports is justifiable; standards of procedure in this area are important to avoid harmful effects for the institutions and persons studied, and political misuse of research findings is always possible. But there can be an over-emphasis and mis-direction of effort, and reflecting on the nature of the research task would seem a more productive course for the incipient evaluation cohort than intruding too far into the realms of school, local authority, or national government decision-making.

Speizman (1974) surely has a point in asserting that 'evaluators' use the methods of other disciplines but claim to have no responsibility to the canons of procedure because they are not involved in basic research. This laxity does not stop them claiming that their findings have much to recommend them. In the field of education, much policy-oriented research has contorted itself in a way which leaves it unable to recognize its inherent weaknesses. Half of Stake's (1976) OECD publication on evaluation deals with 'negotiation of agreements to do evaluation studies' and includes three hypothetical conversations between prospective evaluators and their sponsors. Simons (1977a, 1977b) dwells on negotiation with participants and MacDonald (1977) in the same volume deals with the provocativeness of realism and portrayal. Where, though, is the serious discussion about method, cross-checks, reliability, reservations, and so on?

Policy-oriented research for educational development

I am arguing that so-called evaluation does not hold together as a coherent field of study. Measurement specialists, at least in terms of publications, are in the minority while 'illuminative research' has a counter-culture, 'challenge to academia' aura even encouraged by the people involved, as Stenhouse points out (1979). The field is broad and lacks structures and standards and a determination to establish them.

Several attempts at demarcating the field have been made. Stufflebeam (1969) directs attention to context, input, process and product. Stake goes further and advises:

As evaluators we should make a record of all the following:
What the author or teacher or school etc intends to do,
What is provided in the way of an environment,
The transactions between teacher and learner,

The student progress,
The side effects,
and last and most important, the merit and shortcomings seen by persons from divergent viewpoints.

This is an incomplete list of tasks which potentially fall within the scope of the enquiry. But consider even here the expertise required of one person or a small team – document analysis, interviewing, classroom observation (naturalistic or interaction analysis), testing – and when one comes to analysing the 'side effects' or 'an environment', one is into the whole realm of social science methodology and conceptualization. That policy-oriented research in the curriculum area should have arrived so late at a grasp of the importance of 'side effects' and unanticipated consequences underlines its immaturity; sociologists have long been tuned in to notions of disfunctions, latent function, power and conflict (Merton, 1957). Project development, dissemination, implementation, resulting learning outcomes, even historical and socio-cultural contexts deserve the attention of researchers. The range of relevant enquiries is extensive. How the enquiry is pursued will depend on its required scope, whether it is short-term or long-term, snapshot or longitudinal, predictive or *post hoc*, and on the available (hopefully proven disciplinary) skills of the enquiry team.

The locus of present debates on curriculum reform is not how to develop new programmes but how to get them into operation in schools in ways developers intend. Hence the popularity of on-site investigations of the use to which curriculum projects are put. Illuminative approaches are considered particularly apt in this area. But the arguments about the need for disciplinary procedures and skills are true also of theories and conceptualizations found in the disciplines – and here I refer most particularly to sociology.

Understanding schooling

Some training in social science theory must help the researcher to penetrate beyond the superficial. For instance, to lay great stress on the surface views of participants is to fail to exploit the situation fully and to ignore the fact that such views are situationally located; such views arise and are legitimated within a context, and failure to delve into the wider perspectives of teachers' understanding, can lead to research conclusions which are restricted if not misguided. The interviewer who elicits such comments as 'I couldn't use that technique with my mob' or 'That went down well' must gain an appreciation of how 'my mob' is perceived, how other classes are characterized. 'Went down well' is in need of explication, for instance in the context of what the teacher in practical terms is out to achieve with a class.

The need to look, in Parlett and Hamilton's (1976) terms, at the 'instructional package' within the 'learning milieu' is clear. The problem is the lack of understanding of the milieu. As Sarason (1971) writes:

> There is a surprising degree of similarity between the outsider who wants change and the insider who has a similar goal: both the insider and outsider show an amazing degree of ignorance about the culture of the schools and (equally as fateful) both seem to have no theory of the change process. (p. 2)

There is glib talk about schooling for initiation (Peters, 1966), cultural transmission (Hoyle, 1969), for cognitive, affective (Bloom, 1956), social and emotional development, yet these are *assumptions* about what happens in schools. We even have theses about human capital and preparation for later occupational productivity, and education is one scapegoat for our modern ills, from football hooliganism to economic decline. All this in spite of the fact that the link between education and productivity has consistently been 'not proven' (Berg, 1973) and most research findings indicate that great expenditure on compensatory education programmes has affected by not one jot the life chances of the socio-economically deprived (Little and Smith, 1971). We are aware of the 'root and branch conservatism of teachers' (Husen, 1965) and of the 'persistence of recitation'; Hoetke and Ahlbrand (1969) ask why such a discredited method should remain popular in the face of more highly recommended methods and suggest that it uniquely meets certain survival needs of teachers. Schmuck and Runkel (1971) write that school goals are:

> stated so vaguely by school personnel that they cannot be recognised even when they are being reached . . . Some observers, for example, have concluded that despite quite different verbalised goals, schools in general strive primarily to achieve a quiet and highly predictable order or comportment – typically referred to as the custodial function of schools.

And it cannot even be shown that trained teachers are better than untrained ones (Morrison and McIntyre, 1969).

Thus, although Jean Rudduck (1976) can say that the work of M.F.D. Young 'has crept steadily into consciousness, even the conscience of the teaching world', such works are sought little by new wave evaluators as an input to their own conjectures. We are left with holistic goal-free evaluators armed with great sensitivity and alertness providing some portrayal, information, maybe insight and understanding. But such work operates with surprisingly conventional notions of social and educational life and is, theoretically, severely myopic. There is a need to question our taken-for-granted assumptions about the nature of schooling, in phenomenological terms to go beyond the 'natural' stance, which 'consists primarily in taking the standpoint of commonsense' and adopt the 'theoretic stance [which] consists in standing back from common-sense and studying commonsense to determine its nature' (Apple, 1976). It could be instructive, in enquiring into the broad impact of a project on a school and classroom to, for instance, take note of the fact that pupils are 'labelled' (Hargreaves *et al.*, 1975) and treated according to their ascribed label, that questioning in a lesson might be to 'ensure that it is a pupil's attention not his 'intelligence' or knowledge that is being tested' (Hammersley, 1976), and that causing learning to take place might be a minor concern in the face of control or certification, i.e. examination demands.

There are innumerable possibilities that might be explored by such a bracketing of everyday understanding. The point is that exponents of case studies, descriptive accounts and illuminative reports in evaluative research operate with epistemological assumptions which are not explicit. Amongst the most important of these assumptions is that teachers are committed to generating learning in all the pupils for whom they have responsibility. Numerous works suggest that operating with a suspension of this particular belief (Waller (1965), Jackson (1968), Lortie (1975), Dreeben (1969), Keddie (1971), Sharp and Green (1975), Woods (1979)), research could be most instructive in studies of educational processes and change.

That the school-based problems of utilizing the output of curriculum development projects be investigated is indeed urgent and justifies all the attention being paid to it. The 'rampant conceptual poverty about change processes in general' (Gross *et al.*, 1972) and an inadequate comprehension of what schools are, and how they work, leads too often to simplistic contentions about a mismatch between the proposals of curriculum development teams and the realities of the teacher's world.

Charisma and style

To return to a consideration of the present trend in evaluative research and question why theories *of* evaluation rather than theories *in* evaluation have come to the fore, it is the contention here, of course, that had there been more systematic attempts to evolve and apply more clearly developed models of schooling, the explanatory power of the enquiries would have been much enhanced. I have argued elsewhere about the weaknesses of holistic and illuminative evaluation as it at present exists (Parsons, 1976); two of the foremost British examples, the SAFARI (1974, 1977) and UNCAL (1975) evaluations (MacDonald *et al.*, 1975), have enough critics at base (Elliot, 1977) and acknowledge their dubious service to decision-makers (CERI, no date) sufficiently for detailed appraisal to be unnecessary.

A point of some importance, however, is the *personal qualities* that such evaluations are seen to call for, rather than the application of research skills and theories. MacDonald's writings emphasize politics, ethics and fairness to all through 'democratic evaluation' and negotiation. A recent CERI paper (1975) on evaluation, part of a programme to which Robert Stake made substantial contributions, talks of 'the importance of selecting a leader for the team whose *style* will fit with the range of information required' (CERI, 1975). 'Style' indicates more accurately than the writer knew the tendency for the 'whole person', his character and manner, to be what is presented to and evaluated by a sponsor. The result is a relegation of the importance of specific discipline-related skills and expertise. One is reminded very much of Richard Sennett's 'The Fall of Public Man' (1977), in which he puts forward an antithesis to Riesmann's 'Lonely Crowd' (1950). Against Reismann's view that modern man relates to his fellows according to role, position and universalistic criteria, Sennett argues that 'people are working out in terms of personal feelings, public matters which properly can be dealt with only through codes of impersonal meaning' (p. 5). A political leader is spoken of as 'credible' or 'legitimate' in terms of what kind of man he is rather than in terms of the actions and programmes he espouses. This obsession with 'authenticity', 'intimacy' and 'radical subjectivity' according to Sennett characterizes the contemporary condition; in the field of curriculum change, it would certainly seem to have ousted disciplined skill and scholarly application. But maybe in developing new fields this is to be the case.

The role of the evaluator as espoused by MacDonald, full of seductive nuance though it is, elevates the power and control of the investigator unjustifiably. To act 'as a broker in exchanges of information groups who want knowledge of each other' (MacDonald, 1976, p. 134) makes the investigator a politician and arbiter, roles not easily allied to that of dispassionate information seeker. Coleman (1972) would seem to have a more 'authentic' and less obtuse position regarding policy research (and its place in 'the world of action'), which he distinguishes from unfettered 'discipline research':

> acceptance of the research problem, an act that is still within the world of action, should be governed by the investigator's personal values, not disciplinary values of objectivity and truth. Both the willingness to accept the problem for study and the establishment of conditions of transmitting research results back into the world of action should be governed by these personal values. The execution of the research then must be governed by disciplinary values, which regard the investigator's own personal values and interests no more highly than those of other interested parties. Finally, the transmission back into the world of action must be conceived in two parts: first, reporting of research results, which must be done objectively and openly according to the discipli-

nary values; and second, expression and use of those research results in the world of action. In the latter part, the person who carried out the investigation may be an advocate, just as can any other person in the world of action. In the former, he cannot, any more than he can in the execution of the research. It may be difficult to separate these two capacities, but it is necessary to do so. For if it is not done, then the policy research loses its value for all interested parties. (p. 14)

Here is a position which is sensible, disciplined and the outcome of long deliberation within social research. It clashes horribly with the following naive conception of 'goal free evaluation':

in which a team investigate a process without considering either the administrator's special needs for information or the stated objectives of the process to be evaluated. What emerges is a full picture of the process as seen by the evaluation team, unbiased by any preconceptions – except indeed those of the team themselves. Conceivably situations can arise when there is controversy within an administration when an evaluation of this type, being free from outside pressures, could be useful – *subject only to the difficulty of selecting an evaluator*! (CERI, 1975, p. 9, my emphasis)

Where does evaluation go from here, or would it be best if it disappeared in such a form?

Where there is this dependence on the *person* of the researcher rather than his training or social science competence it signifies a divorce from the research community. This is nowhere better epitomized than in Walker's recent paper, 'On the Uses of Fiction in Educational Research' (1979). Whatever 'process of testing' (p. 7) a fictional account may go through, however it may capture the flavour of the reality experienced by the researcher, it defies authentication. It is a duty of researchers to reveal to an audience the way data were collected and demonstrate stringency in analysis. Walker – incidentally, one of the contributors to Stake and Easley's (1978) *Case Studies in Science Education* – holds an extreme position even within new wave evaluation. By journalistic and literary standards it outshines much educational research but it sacrifices so much for these advantages that its reliability, and hence utility for decision-makers, must be questioned.

Conclusion

Policy-oriented research in education is much needed, as in other fields of public service. As Goodlad (1977) says, 'There is only one honest answer to the question, "What goes on in our schools?" It is that our knowledge is exceedingly limited' (p. 3). However, the term 'evaluation' to describe the research we need has been improperly used, denoting a social or administrative process from which the educational researcher is best excluded. Information requirements of decision-makers should be turned into research questions and pursued according to disciplinary values, the enterprise being considered contract, policy-oriented or policy research.

Further, the debate, even schism, between 'traditional' and 'non-traditional' evaluators has been unhelpful since the more recently advocated modes of enquiry are not substitutes for measurement programmes of pupils' outcomes. However important we might regard studies of process – how schools are organized, how teachers teach, the nature of pupil activity – we are still interested in the results in terms of pupils' development.

The area of enquiry opened up by the proponents of the new styles of evaluation, though important and with exciting propects, is vast and requires a range of skills and knowledge which no small team can pretend to have mastered. This potential breadth of enquiry and its disciplinary roots has scarcely been conceptualized by the 'new evaluators'. Moreover, the understandings of schools and schooling with which such policy researchers operate is, in theoretical terms, inadequate, concentrating on surface features with little heed to deeper contextual features which underpin the behaviour of the social actors. This new style, still in its ascendancy, depends for its reputation and enactment on personal skills rather than professional or disciplinary expertise. Fancy-free, with few disciplinary ties, it must prove itself soon, flop or make the transition to a non-specialist advisory service, where reportage is a legitimate replacement for systematically gathered and analysed data.

The point is that evaluation can most profitably be relocated in discipline-based, policy-oriented research. Even those conducting measurement programmes and controlled experiments could better be seen as contract researchers rather than evaluators; their results could be interpreted as '*According to these criteria or measurements*, A is superior to B,' or 'Under these conditions these objectives were attained'. The decision-makers, whoever they be, must evaluate this evidence, weigh the importance of the advantages of A, and act.

Other researchers less closely tied by preconceived criteria are in the business of advancing understanding. This, in a similar way, aspires to aid decision-making. Science, measurement or humanistic fact-finding cannot solve the normative problems of decision-making but can raise the standards and reliability of factual evidence which constitute *one* input into the decision-making process. I rather like the title of one of Rippey's papers 'When the roll is called up yonder will evaluators be there?' (1973, p. 85). But I think such other-worldly concerns should not distract us from the possibility that evaluators might be called to account rather earlier.

The Plowden Report (HMSO, 1967) recognizes the art in teaching but suggests it would benefit from 'intellectual stiffening'. Similar admonishment can be levelled at what has gone under the title of 'evaluation'; 'soft' evaluation need not be flabby. Policy-oriented research closely allied to the social sciences should be of great benefit particularly at a time when we are experiencing tensions between pressures for greater participation in educational policy-making and greater centralized accountability.

References

Anderson, R. B. (1977) The effectiveness of Follow Through: evidence from the national analysis. *Curriculum Inquiry* **7** (3), 209–26.
—— (1978) Pardon us, but what was the question again? Response to the critique of the Follow Through Evaluation. *Harvard Educational Review* **48** (2), 161–70.
Apple, M. W. (1976) Commonsense and the curriculum. In R. Dale *et al*. (eds.) *Schooling and Capitalism*. London: Routledge & Kegan Paul with the Open University Press.
Bennett, C.A. & Lumsdaine, A.A. (1975) *Evaluation and Experiment*. New York: Academic Press.
Berg, I. (1973) *Education and Jobs*. Harmondsworth: Penguin Education.
Bloom, S. B. (1956) *Taxonomy of Educational Objectives*. 1. *Cognitive Domain*. London: Longman.
Bock, G., Stebbins, L.B. & Proper, E.C. (1977) *Education as Experimentation: A Planned Variation Model*, vol. IVB, *Effects of Follow Through Models*. Cambridge, Mass.: Abt Associates, Inc.
Bogatz, G. A. & Ball, S. (1971) *The Second Year of Sesame Street: A Continuing Education*. New Jersey Educational Testing Service.
Burstall, C. *et al*. (1975) *Primary French in the Balance*. Slough: NFER.
CERI (no date) *The UNCAL Evaluation of Computer Assisted Learning in Case Studies in the Evaluation of*

Educational Programmes, ed. R. E. Stake. Paris: OECD.

—— (1975) *The Use, Commissioning, Implementation and Reporting of Evaluation Studies*. Paris: OECD.

—— (1976) *Evaluating Educational Programmes: The Need and the Response*, prepared by R. E. Stake. Paris: OECD.

Cicerelli, V. G. (1972) In P. H. Rossi & W. Williams (eds.) *Evaluating Social Programmes*. New York: Seminar Press.

Coleman, J. S. (1972) *Policy Research in the Social Sciences*. Morristown, New Jersey: General Learning Press.

Cooper, K. (1976) Curriculum evaluation: definitions and boundaries. In Tawney (1976).

Doe, B. (1976) What about the after eights? *The Times Educational Supplement*, 5 March 1976.

Dreeben, R. (1969) *On What is Learned in Schools*. Reading, Mass.: Addison-Wesley.

Eggleston, J. F. (1976) *Processes and Products of Science Teaching*. London: Macmillan Education.

Elliot, J. (1977) Democratic Evaluation as social criticism: or putting the judgement back into evaluation. In SAFARI 1977, 191–204.

Eraut, M.R. & Collier, K.G. (1979) *Evaluating the New BEd*. London: Society for Research into Higher Education.

Goodlad, J. I. (1977) What goes on in our schools. *Educational Research* 6 (3), 3–6.

Grobman, H. (1968) *Evaluation Activities of Curriculum Projects*. New York: Rand MacNally.

Gross, N. *et al.* (1972) *Implementing Organizational Innovations*. Harper International Education. New York: Harper & Row.

Halsey, A. M. (1972) *Educational Priority*, vol. 1. London: HMSO.

Hammersley, M. (1976) The mobilisation of pupil attention. In M. Hammersley & P. Woods (eds.) *The Process of Schooling*. London: Routledge & Kegan Paul with the Open University.

Hargreaves, D. H. *et al.* (1975) *Deviance in the Classroom*. London: Routledge & Kegan Paul.

HMSO (1967) *Children and Their Primary Schools* (Plowden Report).

Hoetke, J. & Ahlbrand, W. P. (1969) The persistence of recitation. *American Educational Research Journal* **6**, 147–64.

House, E. R. (1974) *The Politics of Educational Innovation*. Berkeley, Calif.: McCutchan.

—— *et al.* (1978) No simple answer: critique of the Follow Through Evaluation. *Harvard Educational Review* **48**(2).

Hoyle, E. (1969) *The Role of the Teacher*. London: Routledge & Kegan Paul.

Husen, T. (1965) Address to the Association for the Advancement of Educational Research.

Jackson, P. W. (1968) *Life in Classrooms*. New York: Holt, Rinehart & Winston.

Jencks, C. *et al.* (1972) *Inequality: A Reassessment of the Effects of Family and Schooling in America*. New York: Basic Books.

Jenkins, D. (1977) Saved by the bell. In D. Hamilton *et al. Beyond the Numbers Game*. London: Macmillan Education.

Keddie, N. (1971) The social basis of classroom knowledge. In M. F. D. Young *Knowledge and Control*. London: Collier-Macmillan.

Kennedy, M. M. (1977) The Follow Through Programme. *Curriculum Enquiry* **7** (3).

Little, A. & Smith, G. (1971) *Strategies of Compensation: A Review of Educational Projects for the Disadvantaged in the United States*. Paris: OECD.

Lortie, D. C. (1975) *Schoolteacher: A Sociological Study*. University of Chicago Press.

McDill, E.L. *et al.* (1972) Evaluation in practice: compensatory education. In P. M. Rossi & W. Williams (eds.) *Evaluating Social Programs*. New York: Seminar Press.

MacDonald, B. (1976) Evaluation and the Control of Education. In Tawney (1976), 125–36.

—— (1977) The portrayal of persons as evaluation data. In SAFARI 1977, 50–67.

MacDonald, B. & Rudduck, J. (1971) Curriculum research and development projects: barriers to success. *British Journal of Educational Psychology* **41** (2), 148–54.

—— *et al.* (1975) *The Programme at Two*. Centre for Applied Research in Education, University of East Anglia.

Makins, V. (1978) Headstart – alive, well and kicking back, *The Times Educational Supplement*, 17 March 1978.

Merton, R. K. (1957) *Social Theory and Social Structure*. New York: Free Press.

Morrison, A. & McIntyre, D. (1969) *Teachers and Teaching*. Harmondsworth: Penguin Education.

Orlans, H. (1973) *Contracting for Knowledge*. San Francisco, Calif.: Jossey Bass.

Parlett, M. & Hamilton, D. (1976) Evaluation as illumination. In Tawney (1976).

Parsons, C. (1976) The new evaluation: a cautionary note. *Journal of Curriculum Studies* **8** (2), 125–38.

Peters, R. S. (1966) *Ethics and Education*. London: Allen & Unwin.

Riesmann, D. (1950) *The Lonely Crowd*. New Haven, Conn.: Yale University Press.

Rippey, R. M. (1973) *Studies in Transactional Evaluation*. Berkeley, Calif.: McCutchan.

Rossi, P.H. & Williams, W. (eds.) (1972) *Evaluating Social Programs*. New York: Seminar Press.

Rudduck, J. (1976) The Humanities Curriculum Project. *Dialogue, Schools Council Newsletter* No. 22.

SAFARI (1974) *Interim Papers: Innovation, Evaluation Research and the Problem of Control*. Centre for Applied Research in Education, University of East Anglia.

SAFARI (1977) *Papers Two: Theory in Practice*. Centre for Applied Research in Education, University of East Anglia.

Sarason, S. B. (1971) *The Culture of the School and the Problem of Change*. Boston: Allyn & Bacon.

Schmuck, R. A. & Runkel, P. J. (1971) *Handbook of Organization Development in Schools*. California: National Press Books.

Scriven, M. (1967) The methodology of evaluation. In R. Taylor *et al*. *Perspectives on Curriculum Evaluation* AERA. Chicago: Rand McNally.

Sennett, R. (1977) *The Fall of Public Man*. Cambridge: CUP.

Sharp, R. & Green, A. (1975) *Education and Social Control*. London: Routledge & Kegan Paul.

Simons, H. (1977a) Building a social contract: negotiation and participation in condensed field research. In SAFARI (1977).

—— (1977b) Conversation piece: the practice of interviewing in case study research. In SAFARI (1977).

Speizman, W.L. (1974) Evaluation from a sociological perspective. In *The Seventy-Third Yearbook of the National Society for the Study of Education*.

Stake, R. (1967) The countenance of educational evaluation. *Teachers' College Record* **68** (7).

—— & Easley (1978) *Case Studies in Science Education*, Booklets 0–15. Centre for Instructional Research and Curriculum Evaluation and Committee on Culture and Cognition, University of Illinois.

Steadman, S.D., Parsons, C. & Salter, B.G. (1978, 1980) *First and Second Interim Reports of the 'Impact and Take-Up Project'*. University of Sussex.

Stenhouse, L. (1979) The problems of standards in illuminative research. *Scottish Education Review* **11**(1).

Stufflebeam, D. (1969) Evaluation as enlightenment for decision-makers. In W. H. Beatty *Improving Educational Assessment*. Washington: Association for Supervision and Curriculum Development.

—— *et al*. (1971) *Educational Evaluation and Decision-Making*, *Phi Kappa Delta*. Itasca, Ill.: Peacock Publishers.

Suchman, A.E. (1967) *Evaluative Research*. New York: Russell Sage.

Tawney, D. (ed.) (1976) *Curriculum Evaluation Today: Trends and Implications*. Schools Council Research Studies. London: Macmillan.

Tyler, R. W. (1949) *Basic Principles of Curriculum and Instruction*. University of Chicago Press.

Walker, R. (1974) The conduct of educational case study: ethics, theory and procedures. In SAFARI (1974).

—— (1979) On the uses of fiction in educational research. Paper given at the Annual Conference of the British Educational Research Association.

Waller, W. W. (1965) *The Sociology of Teaching*. New York: John Wiley.

Warburton, F. W. & Southgate, V. (1969) *i.t.a.: An Independent Evaluation*. London: Murray Chambers.

White, J. P. (1971) The concept of curriculum evaluation. *Journal of Curriculum Studies* **3** (2), 101–12.

Wiseman, S. & Pidgeon, D. (1970) *Curriculum Evaluation*. Slough: NFER.

Woods, P. (1979) *The Divided School*. London: Routledge & Kegan Paul.

3 An eclectic approach to evaluation

Norman Williams

In recent years, there has grown up a widespread questioning of educational methods and achievements, coupled with an increased stress on accountability. This is by no means confined to those who are professionally concerned with education, as is instanced by the press and public response to Bennett's study of teaching styles and pupil achievement and to the HMI report on primary schools. In a different way, the work of the APU is another example of the same concern. In this climate of opinion, the evaluation of educational developments is particularly important.

Such bodies as the Schools Council, with its specially appointed evaluators, and the Open University, with its developmental testing programmes, have provided examples of what may be described as *formal evaluation*, that is to say, evaluation of specific educational developments, carried out by specially appointed individuals or teams. The importance of what takes place in such formal evaluations does, however, go beyond the work they were set up to examine. A good deal of educational writing which is not specifically concerned with evaluation, or at any rate is not labelled as such, nevertheless contains a strong evaluative element. There is now a sizeable literature on the hidden curriculum, which asserts that certain aspects of classroom organization and practice have an additional influence which goes beyond, or in some cases even contradicts, the manifest content of the curriculum. Such work is in fact an evaluative commentary on these aspects of the teachers' work, a point which will be returned to in a later example. The recent emphasis on school-based in-service education of teachers frequently carries with it elements of self-evaluation and of classroom-based curriculum development which, in turn, must be evaluated. It can further be argued that the concept of accountability itself implies the necessity for evaluation, since if there were no valid ways to evaluate the performance of the pupil, the teacher or the school, there would seem to be little possibility of the notion of accountability being translated into practice.

In these circumstances, the assumptions and − more importantly − the practices of professional evaluators are crucial. They provide not only a methodological model which may be adopted by those carrying out less formal evaluations, but also a frame of reference against which such activities may be judged.

The purpose of this paper is to take a fresh look at some of the recent changes in fashion in educational evaluation, to look at some of the causes which may have accounted for them and to argue for a return to a genuinely eclectic approach to evaluation which will include a greater degree of objectivity than has been apparent in some recent studies. The argument is not that there should be a return to earlier purely psychometric and experimental approaches (though, since we are discussing eclecticism, it should be pointed out that there remain areas to which such methods will still be appropriate) but that we need an awareness of the danger that illuminative and social anthropological models, as they are frequently (and wrongly) understood may in the last resort lead only to subjectivism.

Perhaps this statement should be expanded. It is not asserted that evaluation should concern itself only with objective, quantifiable data. Indeed, a wide-ranging evaluation is a complex process which is concerned with answering questions of many kinds. Some of these questions are such that empiricism cannot provide an appropriate basis for an answer. An evaluation, for example, may include some discussion of the nature and value of the aims of the development. Such discussion should be rational, well-informed and conceptually coherent, but it is difficult to see any way in which questions of this sort can be answered by empirical enquiries. An example of such a problem may be seen in Wilson's (1968) discussions of the criteria for moral education in which he decided on conceptual grounds what moral education ought to consist of and argued that many then existing programmes which bore that title were in fact more concerned with social adjustment or religious instruction. Discussion was concerned largely with conceptual analysis, and it is difficult to see how else it could have proceeded. Again, consider the aims of religious education as stated in the Schools Council Working Paper 44 (1972). The authors state that the only legitimate aim of religious education in state schools is to help children to understand religion rather than to help make children religious. They quote with approval the Social Morality Council (1970):

> It is not the purpose of RE . . . to bring about a commitment to the Christian faith, but rather to help children to understand what the Christian faith means in the context of other beliefs sincerely held by men and women of integrity and good will . . .

As is pointed out in the Working Paper, 'a few teachers reject this point of view and say bluntly that they regard it as their duty to instil Christian belief into the children in their charge'. The authors counter this argument by asserting that such objectors are 'acting as evangelists rather than teachers, and as missionaries rather than educators. They were appointed as teachers, and it is important that they should be faithful to their appointment and accept their role as educationalists'.

The point is this: for the few objectors quoted, an empirical enquiry about the extent to which a religious education programme is able to achieve the ends suggested in the Working Paper would be totally irrelevant, since in their view it is the ends themselves which are unacceptable. A dispute concerning differing values must be settled by argument and rational analysis rather than experimental enquiry (if indeed it can be settled at all in the sense of the differing interests becoming reconciled in a common programme). On the other hand, there are other aspects of an evaluation which cannot conceivably be undertaken without reference to empirical data. If the evaluator is interested in the possible implementation of a programme, the question of cost becomes important. It would be surprising if it were to be suggested that the cost of materials, say, were to be assessed on the basis of analysis of the interactions in a group discussion rather than by consulting the publisher's price list. Of course, even here, more complex associated questions may arise. We may wish to know not merely how much the materials cost but whether they are worth the money. In this case we may well return to a discussion of teachers' impressions and experiences.

Evaluation, then, is not a single process; it is not even concerned in every case with providing answers to the same kind of question. It is not possible, therefore, to make generalized statements about appropriate methods which will be applicable to all cases. To do so would be to run the risk of making simplistic and naive statements about the methods to be adopted which, being applied to all aspects, would certainly be inappropriate in some cases. What we cannot afford is the development of a new orthodoxy whereby some techniques may be universally accepted on doctrinal grounds irrespective of context, and others rejected as heresies. Exclusive reliance on a single approach is rarely a characteristic of a well-conducted evaluation.

The first approaches to curriculum evaluation tended to suffer from such a tendency to simplism. They were for the most part derived from experimental methods which had their origins in research in the social and biological sciences. Evaluators have more recently almost abandoned this approach. Many reasons were given at the time to justify this change in direction. Among them is the statement that such evaluation too frequently failed to produce results which were statistically significant. It is quite true that summative evaluations which used this model could be singularly frustrating to the curriculum developers whose work was being evaluated. All too often they would put three or more years' work into the development of materials, only to be told by the evaluator that the materials did not produce any outcomes other than those which could be ascribed to random variation in test scores.

However, even though the results of such evaluations could be frustrating, the traditional experimentalist might judge the abandoning of his method to be a strange reaction, as though the curriculum developers and evaluators were saying 'the tests did not support us, so we will scrap the tests'. At first sight, it would appear that the procedure is unexceptionable. The earlier workers were concerned with a relatively simple matter: any curriculum project had aims and objectives; the attainment of such aims and objectives must be accompanied by changes in, for instance, performance, behaviour or attitude. All that is required is the construction of a measuring instrument which will reflect such changes in order to measure the outcome of a trial of the materials, preferably in a classical experimental method incorporating experimental and control groups, and to allow, in the interpretation of the results, for such changes as may occur due to the random variations in repeated tests. Our classical experimentalist would say that to abandon the method of verification rather than to go back to the drawing board is a solution which would be clearly unacceptable in development programmes in other fields. In fact, of course, it was not so lacking in justification as might appear to the experimentalist. On closer examination, it can be shown that there are a number of valid reasons for choosing a new direction. Such reasons of course are not necessarily historical reasons in the sense that they were advanced by those involved in the field at the time, but, perhaps with the benefit of hindsight, they show that a change was justifiable in principle.

The earlier approaches were not only characterized by an experimental approach; there was also a great deal of reliance on psychometrics. It was rarely the case, however, that standardized measures which exactly fitted the problem under consideration were already available, since the projects were dealing with new approaches. Hence, two choices were open to the evaluator: either a properly standardized instrument which did not exactly fit the problem could be used, or new scales could be developed which related more closely to the project's predicted outcome. Both choices had disadvantages. Previously standardized instruments generally had good reliability and a high validity for the attribute for which the test was originally designed. However, since this would relate only in part to the attribute which the evaluator wished to test, any effects arising from the use of project materials could easily be swamped by variance arising from other factors. Equally, the use of *ad hoc* scales had difficulties: rigorous establishment of discrimination, reliability and validity is a very time consuming process, and this was a largely unattainable goal in practice when viewed against the life cycle of most projects. *Ad hoc* scales of this sort tended, therefore, to be characterized by a number of undesirable features which could include low reliability, excessive variability and doubtful validity.

In the analysis of the results, statistical significance was usually tested by parametric procedures, such techniques as the t-test being typical of the earlier approaches. In such measures, of course, the magnitude of the gain scores, or the difference between means, is only one factor in the computation of the significance level, which may be lowered by factors intrinsic to the test itself, such as its variability. We see therefore that we are dealing with the familiar question of type one and type two errors. In one case we are failing to observe an effect which is only present in the classroom and in the other we seem to be detecting tendencies where none exist (only perhaps random variations such as may occur between any two observations). One may also point to the tendency to use parametric statistics to handle test results when the tests were such that the necessary assumptions about the nature and distribution of the scores could not be made. The analysis of data by parametric statistics demands that a number of criteria relating to any measures used must be met. These include the need for the measures to be on, at the least, an equal interval scale and more importantly that the distribution of the results conforms to the normal distribution graph. We have seen above that the time constraints within which a typical evaluator must operate may preclude these criteria being met. In such cases the application of these traditional statistical methods must be at the least deferred, and it is much safer to employ statistics which do not rest upon such assumptions. Very well known examples of such statistics are chi-squared and rank order correlations.

There are other reasons why the classical experimental approach may be limited in its application. Many educational programmes have long-term aims and objectives. It can be argued for instance that the Health Education project cannot objectively be said to have achieved its aims until we have information about the mental and physical health of students who have been exposed to it, information leading well into their adult lives and including, possibly, information on how they will fulfil their future role as parents. Information of this sort is beyond the reach of the short-term classical study, and in any case, by the time it is available, the materials will be very likely out of date and the project replaced by a new approach. But the unavailability of long-term information does not imply that we must retreat to a position of subjectivism leavened by optimism and, indeed, the Schools Council Health Education projects have devoted a good deal of time to the development of worthwhile objective indicators of the effectiveness of their materials.

Thus, those evaluators who argued for the need of a new approach were reacting against a method which could be validly criticized and which had real difficulties. The question to be considered, however, is whether disenchantment with the former techniques has led to a practice in which qualitative perception has replaced objective data and its analysis to such an extent that the latter is either not sought for in the first place or is unreported even when it would in principle be available. It must be stressed at this point that this is not intended as a criticism of such writers as Parlett and Hamilton whose definition of the task of the illuminative evaluator fits in very closely to what is here referred to as an eclectic approach to evaluation. They argue that no single technique can serve all evaluative tasks and that the evaluator has to choose the most useful approach or approaches to find the answer to a particular problem. The use of objective data is certainly not excluded by these authors. What is asserted however is that as Tall (1978) says: 'The contrast between this and the earlier emphasis on measurement has sometimes led to the assumption of a dichotomy between "illuminators" and "measurers".' Recent examples of work which has been influenced by illuminative evaluation reveal an attitude which is often frankly hostile to objective data and places an excessive reliance on subjective criteria. It is not the work of Parlett and Hamilton then which is at issue but rather what has been made of this by some of the people who have taken up their ideas. It is however worth pointing out that any methodology should nevertheless be sufficiently robust to provide at least an adequate level of evaluation when used by less distinguished workers in the field.

We shall go on to look at examples which illustrate these more recent practices but, before doing so, it is worth noting that in spite of more recently developed hostility to objective measures of the classical kind, there still remains a place for them in many evaluations. Projects with general aims such as the improvement of reading skills, oral skills or numerical ability can properly make use of the standardized test. The Schools Council projects, Effective Use of Reading and Extending Beginning Reading, for instance, necessarily used standardized reading tests in their development and evaluation work, using these in conjunction with other measures such as CLOZE, a procedure in which words are deleted from a text on a regular basis (e.g. every fifth word) and the pupil is required to complete the text thus providing information about his use of the reading material. Where projects are concerned with gains in highly specific skills or pieces of information we may also find it appropriate to assess such gains by objective tests. Part of a maths module may, for instance, be concerned with square roots; a unit in a French course may be concerned with forming and using negatives. Assessment of pupil performance in such cases as this does not require a high degree of sophistication. The way to find out whether pupils can work out square roots is to get them to work out square roots. In such cases, we are concerned with a kind of criterion referenced testing and this forms a proper part of the evaluation.

Examples of work which shuns quantitative methods are not difficult to find. Consider, for instance, the following passage (PLS Dissemination Study Reports from Schools No. 3: Head Teacher's Evaluation, p. 36):

> it was possible to identify the following areas of success . . . The course has initiated an on-going discussion of important issues such as the degree of individual based work possible within our organisation and within the context of our aims, and the purpose and value of record keeping. We are also questioning the balance between our cognitive and behavioural aims.

The passage raised more questions than it answered. What is meant by 'on-going discussion'? How often did it happen? Presumably it refers to something other than the discussions reported in the publication itself, since these groups were set up with the express purpose of discussing, and the comment would therefore necessarily be true of them. Which teachers discussed? Who did not? Was there any effect on practice? Similarly, in the same document, we read: 'The presence of check lists caused some considerable difficulties. Firstly, many teachers felt that they wanted to contribute more towards the construction of their own statements but the very existence of the "ready made" statements was off-putting.' Similar questions are raised by this short extract. How serious are 'considerable' difficulties? How many difficulties were mentioned? The word is used in the plural but in fact only one is reported. Again, what is meant by many teachers? Were they a majority? Questions such as these were not raised to criticize the work of the head teacher concerned since he was following an example set by many evaluation reports. But it remains true that the information sought by the questions could certainly have been obtained. It would also certainly have been relevant to an evaluation of the work of the project in that school.

This tendency is by no means confined to part-time evaluators, such as the head teacher cited above, but may also be discerned in the work of professional curriculum developers. The following passage comes from a report (unpublished at the time of writing) of a major Schools Council project. Though it does not form part of the work of the evaluator of the project, it is interesting as a statement of the evaluation method adopted by other team members for formative self-evaluation.

An integral part of planning a formal curriculum is evaluating whether objectives have been achieved and whether content and method have worked. The project decided against the traditional kind of summative evaluation which concentrates on administering to children quasi-scientific instruments such as attitude scales. Instead we opted for the rough and ready measures any sensitive and experienced teacher could make use of. We observed classrooms – what children wrote, painted, said and did and, above all, how they reacted to the introduction of multiracial themes and materials; and we interviewed children, individually and in pairs and small groups, to see what they had learned or gained and what their opinions were of the curriculum they had experienced. We also, of course, asked teachers for their views. . . . and its effectiveness can be assessed there. Whatever its defects from a strictly scientific point of view, it does attempt to take account of the complexity of life in classrooms, and shows how the 'effective' curriculum of what actually happens, what is actually learned, can furnish the teacher with data for reviewing and revising the formal curriculum of his aims, content and methods. Moreover, in treating children as agents with goals of their own, and opinions to express, rather than merely as objects to be tested and measured, it seeks to embody the important principle of involving them in the control of their own learning. In this respect, at least, we find ourselves at one with the overriding concern of child-centred educational theory that children should become autonomous.

Apart from the fact that it is possible to infer from the second sentence ('quasi-scientific instruments') some degree of hostility to quantified data, there are a number of points which are not dissimilar to those made above. Without entering into a debate as to whether the findings reported represent a fair overall statement of what was discovered, it is possible to assert that a great deal more information could have been provided by the inclusion of quantification. How many classrooms were observed? Where were they and what were they like? How many children and teachers were interviewed? It is stated that the effectiveness of the method can be assessed from the report, but this is precisely what we cannot do. We are dependent on the skill and integrity of those who are writing the report. It is not being suggested that the authors were lacking in integrity and skill, but this is not the point. The reader should not be put in a position of relying on this – a point which will be returned to later. The authors claim that the method attempts to take account of the complexity of life in classrooms, but does it in fact succeed? The opinions reported are unanimous – while this may be a fair representation of the majority view, some indication of the incidence of minority opinions might have provided a more accurate picture of the complexity of classroom life.

We can also make comments of this kind about work which, though not overtly evaluative, is in fact concerned with evaluation. Dale, writing for the Open University in 1976, evaluates certain aspects of the hidden curriculum.

the second grade child realises that some people look different and speak differently from others and that some know more, learn more and have more wealth than others. Differences in wealth seem to be associated with both knowledge and ability and they are treated as phenomena as natural as differences in speech and ability . . . The school . . . effectively taught the social myths necessary to sustain the social class system that was a product of the economic order.

The analyst's political values are quite overt, but these do not excuse him from the need to demonstrate, rather than to assert, that there are latent intentions in school organization, that aspects of these are perceived by the second grade child, and above all that the process is, as is stated, effective.

The examples that we have looked at have moved from an absence of complete and quantified information and reliance on the reporting of overall impressions to outright assertion. Ultimately, such approaches lead to the stance taken up by T. Green in his discussion of Independent Learning in Science at a meeting of the Schools Council Evaluators' Group, where he rejected the idea of objective evaluation in favour of what was referred to as 'gut evaluation'. 'The question is,' he went on, 'whose gut do you trust?' This is indeed the question. It summarizes the disquiet which must be raised by many of the instances referred to above, and as suggested in that context there is a further question, namely, whether the reader ought to be put into the position of having to evaluate the evaluator before he knows what to make of the evaluation. Is it right that our judgement, whether we be funding bodies or potential users, should be dependent on frequently unobtainable information about the personal qualities of the individual who carried out the evaluation? We may regard such evaluation as analogous to literary criticism. This is a situation which may be quite acceptable if we are assessing the judgements of a critic, who provides us with weekly evaluations which provide ample opportunity for the development of a balanced view of their overall appropriateness for the individual reader (and the adverse consequences of a wrong judgement are in any case less serious). An individual educational evaluator's reports do not appear more frequently than once every few years, and we are frequently unable to build up a picture of the track record of the evaluator as critic on a personal basis.

In recent years, increasing stress has been laid on evaluation of the *process* of curriculum development. This is both interesting and important but if pursued as an end in itself the study can become narcissistic. Ultimately, education is about children and their teachers. It may be the case that evaluation which concentrates solely on narrowly defined outcomes omits information which is useful, but evaluation which omits consideration of outcomes altogether is omitting the core of the process. In every case, we need to know how many children were helped by a curriculum development and how many were not. We need to know which kinds of children benefited and how great the benefit was. We also need as much information as possible about the circumstances in which successes and failures respectively occurred. The problem is perhaps not whether this should be done, but how can it be done? It has already been conceded that there are many cases where the traditional psychometric approaches are unable to provide the necessary information, and that we are necessarily dependent on devices such as the collection of teachers' and pupils' impressions. Is it possible to introduce a degree of objectivity into the reporting and analysis of such subjective data?

Perhaps medical research, which has already faced this problem, may provide a useful analogy. It is not suggested that there is necessarily a close correspondence in all aspects between the two areas of enquiry, but some of the problems have sufficient in common to make the impression at the least suggestive. New therapies and drugs are not acceptable without evaluation. As we saw in the case of thalidomide, an oversight in such research is likely to lead to tragedy and a public outcry. The reason for this is quite clear – the consequences of an inadequate medical evaluation are, if not fatal, then frequently dramatic. The consequences in the case of curriculum development are less dramatic, but they can nonetheless be serious. In medical research, as in curriculum development, objective and reliable measures are not always available. It is true that there exist such measures as temperature and blood count, which are reliable in the technical sense, but the researcher into new therapies must also deal with such subjective measures as the disappearance of a headache and other subjectively experienced symptoms, the fact that the patient 'feels better' or is able to do a normal day's work without 'undue fatigue'. In such cases, it is not assumed that the objective approach be altogether abandoned. Where factors cannot be objectively and reliably measured, instances can be counted and tabulated, and an appropriate analysis of the results can be carried out.

This analogy should illuminate our field of curriculum development and illuminate it in an optimistic way. It is true that the earlier psychometric approaches often did not work, but it does not follow that we must on that account retreat into subjectivism. Among our concerns there is inevitably that of the outcome of any curriculum development for the child, and this may not properly be omitted from our consideration. Even though such outcomes are not in all cases objectively measurable, it does not follow that they have no observable consequences. Indeed, if there are no observable consequences, it is difficult to see how it can be asserted that anything has happened. If this is so, then such consequences can be recorded and assigned to categories – even if the categories are as simple as 'observed/not observed' – and the significance of the distribution of such categories can be assessed. As we have seen, nonparametric statistical methods are highly developed and are entirely appropriate for the analysis of such data.

This is not, however, intended as a recipe for a new simplism, a fresh orthodoxy. There is perhaps an inherent tendency in this direction among those whose training has been in the older research disciplines. What is needed, it is felt, is a tighter design, a better methodology whereby all the extraneous factors will be controlled; or, perhaps, the application of ever more sophisticated methods of analysis, improved analyses of variance and the like. In education, the perfect, definitive experiment is a chimera.

To recognize this is not to be pessimistic. In practice, though, it does mean that we cannot rely on a single source or type of data. An evaluation will need to draw on as wide a range of evidence as possible including test scores, teachers' and pupils' opinions, observations and so on. This will permit the evaluator to draw conclusions which rest upon a number of different kinds of data giving a better based conclusion, a process usually referred to as triangulation by analogy with the trigonometrical process. In educational research Occam's Razor may be more powerful than the most sophisticated analyses.

The translation of all this into practice in an evaluation is by no means difficult. There already exists in schools a great deal of evidence which is at once both easily collected and quantifiable. This is particularly true if the evaluator bears in mind the kinds of unobtrusive measures suggested by Webb, Campbell *et al.* (1966). The work of these authors has been available for more than ten years but their approach has not been allowed to make sufficient impact on the work of the educational evaluator. Let us consider two simple illustrations of how this may be achieved in practice. Take, for example, a reading project which includes among its desired outcomes an increase in the amount of reading for pleasure done by the pupils. It is admittedly possible, and it may be useful, to conduct a questionnaire survey of reading habits, or to administer an attitude to reading scale, or to do both of these. Teachers' observations will also be relevant. However, most schools have library records showing the actual number of withdrawals. These figures provide a useful index of the book borrowing habits of the pupils concerned; and it is data which is not expensive to obtain and, as pointed out above, it is susceptible to quantification and objective analysis. It should be stressed again perhaps at this point that what is suggested is not an abandonment of other methods but the addition of extra methods which will provide a reliable and objective basis for triangulation.

Similarly, a module of a health education programme may concern itself with smoking. Evaluation of the effects of this module may well include measures of the degree to which the students have acquired new information and knowledge about smoking and its effects, and their attitudes to tobacco and smoking gathered in interviews and attitude scales of questionnaires (or some combination of these). It would surely not be out of place to include some assessment of the presence or absence of changes in the students' smoking habits. Traditional psychometricians may well opt to explore this outcome by attitude scale and self-report. This data will probably not be without relevance, but it can be supplemented. Most schools have a secluded corner where students disappear for a furtive cigarette. A co-operative school caretaker or cleaner can provide very good information about changes in the number of cigarette ends and discarded cigarette packets found in this area.

An actual example of this approach is provided by the Schools Council project on Graded Tests in Modern Languages which was carried out under the direction of Eric Hawkins of York Language Teaching Centre. The project was in essence an evaluation of certain aspects of the graded examinations movement. Teachers who had been concerned in the development of such tests claimed to have detected a marked improvement on the part of their pupils in their attitude towards French – a suggestion of considerable potential importance in view of the declining numbers in the subject over recent years. The team's brief was to discover whether there was evidence of such an attitude shift. They chose not to rely solely on a clinical experimental study, involving experimental and control groups and a pre and post-test by means of an attitude scale; although this approach was employed (and in this case it yielded highly significant results in favour of the hypothesis) it was supplemented by a number of observations of various kinds. These included a questionnaire to teachers and to parents, interviews with teachers, and the results of the tasks of a working group of teachers who had been involved in the work. In addition, an unobtrusive measure of the kind referred to above was employed which consisted of recording the numbers of pupils in the control and experimental schools who actually opted to continue with French in the fourth year. Again, significant results were found. The agreement which was found between these various measures gave the conclusions of the evaluation a broad base and a consequent strength which is much more impressive than when even a significant difference is obtained on any of these measures alone.

What we are arguing for is the addition and not the substitution of data of this kind to the evaluator's activity. What is needed is a return to a truly eclectic approach to evaluation.

References

Bennett, Neville (1976) *Teaching Styles and Pupil Progress*. London: Open Books.

Dale, R. (ed.) (1976) *Schooling and Capitalism*. London: Routledge & Kegan Paul.

Schools Council (1972) *Religious Education in Primary Schools*, Working Paper 44. London: Evans/Methuen Educational.

Social Morality Council (1970) *Moral and Religious Education in County Schools*.

Webb, E.J. *et al*. (1966) *Unobtrusive Measures: Nonreactive Research in the Social Sciences*. Chicago: Rand McNally.

Williams, N. (ed.) (1978) *An Introduction to Evaluation*. London: Schools Council Publications.

Wilson, J., Williams, N. & Sugerman, B. (1968) *Introduction to Moral Education*. Harmondsworth: Penguin.

4 Accomplishing evaluation: towards a methodology*

David Smetherham

The practice of illuminative evaluation as advocated by
Parlett and Hamilton (1972) has been roundly criticized
for its apparent lack of any rigorous methodology and the
subjective, anecdotal, nature of its reportage. It is seen as
promoting some ill-defined sensitivity and personal quality on the part of the evaluator at the expense of professional research expertise. Parsons (1976; 1980) is typical of
the critics in expounding the need for evaluators to establish some explicit standards of procedure.

In this collection of papers Parsons takes his argument a
stage further and suggests that getting their own house in
order might be viewed as a productive course for what he
calls the incipient evaluation cohort. His main concern,
expressed in the concluding argument of 'A policy for
educational evaluation', is that the ascendant new wave
evaluation research:

   depends for its reputation and enactment on personal

*I am most grateful to Mike Cannon (evaluator of S.C. Careers Pro-
ject), Heather Lyons (evaluator of S.C. Language Across the Third Year
Curriculum Project) and Gordon Elliott for their helpful comments.
Neither these nor the projects with which they were associated are
related to the activities of Doris.

skills rather than professional or disciplinary expertise. Fancy-free, with few disciplinary ties, it must prove itself soon, flop, or make the transition to a non-specialist advisory service, where reportage is a legitimate replacement for systematically gathered and analysed data.

The point is that evaluation can most profitably be relocated in discipline-based, policy-oriented research. (this volume, p.62)

The general argument, with which I have some sympathy, therefore calls for a publicly displayable ground of evidence. However the point at issue, and the point at which I would part company with Parsons, is that whatever personal skills are they are a necessary part of professional expertise. Interestingly enough this would also be true for sociology or whatever social science discipline was used as a base. In evaluation particularly neither discipline base or personal skills can exist independently of each other. In the context of the new wave evaluation the difficulty is that its rather ill-defined operational bases have yet to be systematically explored. Whereas the practice of professional or disciplinary technical expertise has been established for a sufficiently long period for it to be organized, catalogued and indexed, this task of codification has still to be carried out in the area of personal skill.

In this paper the reader is therefore offered a critique of Parsons's position as I understand it. My contention is that the personal/social skills dimension is an important aspect of professional expertise. Accordingly, it ought to be placed in a framework that demonstrates its relevance to more traditional research methodologies. Indeed, consideration of evaluation as a disciplined enquiry holds out considerable potential benefits to both evaluators and their parent disciplines. The meeting of two (or more) research traditions could be expected to aid in the development of the more critical methodology sought by Parsons, yet one in which the evaluation community has something to offer researchers working within more tradi-tional disciplines as well as less traditional ones. The dis-tinction to be drawn is that between an uncritical approp-riation of the technique by the evaluator (except as legitimized in the originating disciplines), and the posses-sion of a sufficient understanding of the method in order to generate further insights and theoretical understandings. An example is provided by Wilson (1977) in his description of the greater or lesser appropriateness of using ethnog-raphic techniques in evaluation research.

Personal quality as disciplined enquiry

In his paper Parsons considers it to be a point of some importance that illuminative evaluations are perceived as calling for personal qualities *rather than* research skills. He argues that, as a consequence, the importance of specific (that is, discipline-related) professional skills and expertise is diminished. Support for such a view can be found in the experience of at least one evaluator researcher (Lyons, 1977). Lyons is unequivocal in believ-ing that the (evaluation) research process can be expected to be involved, almost inevitably, with 'interpersonal ten-sions, rivalries and crises of various sorts *which affected what happened* as well as some striking instances of group cohesion and co-operativeness' (p. 20, my emphasis). This interpersonal dimension is an important aspect of the evaluation research activity and presumably includes what Parsons would identify as personal skills. The quota-tion also rather nicely draws attention to a certain ambivalence in the title of this paper: accomplishing evaluation.

The title owes much to the example provided by young ladies of the Victorian era. Some of the things such young ladies were taught explicitly concerned those social and technical accomplishments thought appropriate to the behaviour of educated ladies holding their position in society. Such accomplishments ranged from the social etiquette of the dance floor to the accomplished needlewoman, from knowing how to behave in society to the keeping of accounts and organizing the smooth operation of a household. The accomplished woman possessed all of these skills, and so personal qualities could not be separated from socio-professional expertise.

There is some tension inherent in this notion of accomplishing a task. Accomplishing evaluation conveys a process, a thinking not-yet-finished. It is here, perhaps, that the process-oriented aspect of accomplishment impinges most directly upon the personal/social skills of the evaluator. Indeed, the actual acquisition of personal and social skills can itself be something of an accomplishment when related to some desired outcome. On the other hand, the accomplishment of evaluation denotes a task that has been fulfilled, an objective that has been achieved. In this sense to speak of accomplishing evaluation – and all that this entails – denotes completeness, and perhaps even includes the notion that the evaluation report has been submitted on time! In talking about the task component inherent in the notion of accomplishing evaluation I would wish to stress that some of the tensions and problems so frequently encountered in evaluation practice are *structural*. They may arise from the very nature of the evaluation research itself regardless of the personal skills of the evaluator. That is, the significance of personal skills is related to the social structure within which the evaluation research takes place, to the task itself and not to any particular method. It is this aspect that is developed in this paper and, in my view, seriously weakens the force of Parsons's argument.

However, just as the accomplishments of our Victorian young ladies could sometimes be superficial or merely ornamental, I am not here concerned to defend an evaluation that *depends* on personal skills *rather than* on professional expertise. What is being suggested is rather that the processes (including any demonstration of personal and social skills) involved in accomplishing an evaluation are intimately linked with the accomplishment (i.e. the product) of that same evaluation. The critics have a point. None the less, it is also true that all research activity is a blending of personal and professional skills. Whilst the precise mixture may vary according to the nature of the activity there is a blend. Practitioners of the new wave evaluation (because it demands that the evaluator /researcher gets involved, and because of its links with decision-makers) are better placed than many other researchers for first teasing out and then sharpening up the socially produced nature of research knowledge. By making the two skills too discrete there is a danger of missing out an important dimension of the evaluation research activity. It is therefore unfortunate, if understandable, that the personal-professional interaction endemic to the evaluation activity has so far tended to remain hidden from both public and scholarly scrutiny.

However, a body of literature is emerging that indicates the issue is beginning to be aired in particular fields of research. Hargreaves (1968) is far from unique in providing the reader with an example of the interactive nature of the research activity. Indeed there are a number of indications that researchers will increasingly feel the need to describe the research process as it is. All the characters are real. Shipman (1976) has edited a series of essays contributed by various educational researchers given the brief to include not only the research design, but the personal and professional problems that had to be overcome. They were asked to describe it as it happened, to include the brains and heart of the research experience which for various reasons, had often been left out of accounts of research work. This concern extends beyond the educational research community to include other social researchers. Bell and Newby (1977) have been responsible for a similar compilation deriving from sociology. Nor is such concern merely a pragmatic thing divorced from any theoretical structure. Gouldner (1972), when arguing for what he terms a reflexive sociology, sees this as insisting that:

> while sociologists desperately require talent, intelligence and technical skill, they also need courage, a valour that may be manifested every day in the most personal and commonplace decisions. . . . a Reflexive Sociology is distinguished by its refusal to segregate the intimate or personal from the public and collective, or the everyday from the occasional 'political' act. It rejects the old-style closed-office politics. A Reflexive Sociology is not a bundle of technical skills – it is a conception of how to live and a total (practice) praxis. (p. 504)

It is almost taken for granted that such essays will be expected to be eminently readable and to possess a ready audience. It is always fascinating for others to glimpse something of another's secret garden. However, if the exercise is to be something more than a good read, a professional voyeurism, the evaluation research community must be prepared to make their own special contribution to the debate and also respond to the outsider's cynical 'so what?' What does it matter, the argument runs, if researchers are now beginning to reveal the task of accomplishing their research as an essentially human enterprise in which the various members are more or less successful in working out their own salvation? After all, in many instances the substance of any research report has long since been incorporated into the literature and duly appears on the appropriate recommended reading lists. Thus, the majority of present readers will doubtless be almost too familiar with Hargreaves's *Social Relations in a Secondary School* and Lacey's *Hightown Grammar*, albeit perhaps less acquainted with the *Schools Council Integrated Studies Project*. The case to be answered is: what dire consequences may follow from *not* having read, for example, the methodological appendix in Hargreaves (1968); or Lacey's (1976) review of the methodology of *Hightown Grammar* or Shipman *et al.*' s (1974) account of life inside a curriculum project?

To the extent that methodology develops from continuous reflection about the practical problems encountered during the conduct of a particular study, then *not* having read these accounts makes for an uninformed and perhaps misinformed evaluation. For example, it appears reasonable to assume some tension in an evaluation concerned to represent the underdog (Elliott, 1977) that is not just about the exercise of personal skill but relates to the wider social structure. In any event, and as Parlett and Hamilton (1972) point out:

> research workers in this area need not only technical and intellectual capability but also interpersonal skills. They seek co-operation but cannot demand it. There may be times when they encounter nervousness and even hostility. They are likely to be observing certain individuals at critical times in their lives (. . . with a high personal investment in the innovation). (p. 26)

The suggestion being explored in this paper is that such tension can be as much structural – and a result of the evaluation research activity – as personal. As such it may presumably be manifested in a number of ways. Elliott's (1977) may be ideological (see also Becker, 1967). Shipman *et al.*'s (1974) references to the need for participation as well as observation which could have led to his consideration as purely a member of the project team were pragmatic and methodological. The point is that such tensions are built in to an evaluation exercise. They may occur later rather than sooner but no amount of personal-social skill will avoid them. Such a methodology could be expected, for example, to draw attention to a possible distinction between the 'macro' and 'micro' aspects of the exercise. The macro-framework provides evaluation research with a sense of direction and invests it with a responsiveness in particular situations, whilst the micro aspects contain those elements that can be modified. It is at this point that the evaluator needs the courage of Gouldner's reflexive methodology: an analytical framework legitimated by a supportive community.

Auditing the accounts

The vast majority of formal evaluations tend to be public exercises funded by an institution which is likely to be particularly sensitive to criticism. It is for this reason that there is a grave concern that evaluation reports *as a genre* are subject to systematic distortion. This is not seen as a particularly radical suggestion and it is interesting to read the respected anthropologist Mary Douglas (1975) making much the same point in the context of anthropology:

> imagine the anthropologist who, fresh home from the field, announces: 'My tribe hasn't got any religion'. There ought to be a Bateman cartoon to illustrate the dropped spectacles and raised eyebrows and the sense of horrid solecism. No one has interest in the news except to pass a harsh verdict on the man's fieldwork.
>
> Pity the poor anthropologist who expected his field-work to yield the usual interesting information on ritual symbolism.
>
> If he comes home without it, his monograph will lack its crowning glory.Knowing this only too well while he is in the field, he works towards a nervous collapse or an angry show-down with his hosts, whom he suspects of holding out on him. How can he be sure that his field-work is not at fault, or that their disinclination to reveal their religion is not due to secretiveness or deep reserve? Will it be a matter of time? Madame Dieterlen said the Dogon only opened up after seven years of intense enquiry, that it took twenty years to get the full story.

If the anthropologist is in a hurry with his career, he cannot be blamed for turning to another problem, land tenure or politics. On this he soon becomes so much an expert that he never has time again to research into primitive religion. Thus unintentionally is a professional bias established. And thus a most interesting subject rendered sterile. (pp. 76 f.)

This general line of argument has a particular relevance for the practitioners of the new wave evaluation. Both disciplined research and evaluation tend to offer a hazardous purchase on problems rather than some safe plateau of professional competence. The difficulty in evaluation is that, ultimately, there is no supporting community: no power base from which to operate. It is this context that Parsons seemingly fails to appreciate when he, in my view mistakenly, attacks the new wave evaluators for undue reliance on personal skills.

In practice it is difficult to see how a lone evaluator can operate procedures at any rational level if his or her very professional existence is threatened by lack of support. And by this I mean support going beyond the intellectual corroboration of his or her activities and findings. If you consider the personal interrelationships extant between the contributors to 'Beyond the Numbers Game', you have an image of people accessible to each other over telephones, working parallel furrows, having their offices in similar institutions, sharing the same defences. It seems a little ironic that a research tradition which has rediscovered the realities of group dynamics in the professional support systems amongst teachers in schools, should have overlooked their significance to its own survival and development! In the absence of such an unassuming support system, it seems to me that one has to be invented, especially if the researchers find themselves 'between schools' and uncertain on power bases. With such support I would imagine that one can more readily make the often necessary acknowledgements of uncertainty in one's own work, and conjecture about this with the relative freedom from anxiety that only operational confidence allows. Without it, it seems equally likely that one will become so liable to confuse the uncertainties of research issues with personal/professional uncertainties that the quality of service to clients and sponsors alike may prove very difficult to maintain.

The practice of evaluation

The general thrust of my argument is that this intermingling of the personal and professional does in fact appeal to an established research tradition. To this extent Parsons's criticism is essentially misconceived. It is possible to locate the practice of personal and social skills quite satisfactorily within a disciplined enquiry paradigm. The task for the new wave evaluator is rather to combine the insights of the evaluator and researcher in an intelligent, eclectic way to the benefit of both.

In order to bring out something of the *structural* origins of the tensions that can be encountered in the practice of evaluation a case study approach will be used as a sort of critical case. The concern will be to sketch out the beginnings of a codification system that allows the issue of personal skills to be incorporated as part of the existing professional expertise. This approach builds upon the experiences of Doris, a fictitious name assumed on behalf of an evaluator, as she copes with the practicalities of actually doing an evaluation, particularly during her first days in the field. Doris is therefore a presentational device that serves to bring the discussion into the realm of practice – how evaluation is actually accomplished. However, although Doris originated from the experiences of evaluating one particular curriculum development project she rapidly became something of an ideal type. In this capacity Doris now represents an amalgam of experiences.

To provide something of the background, the activity

facing Doris is essentially that of making an evaluation of a group of English teachers engrossed in a process of thinking aloud about their classroom practices. These reflections are eventually to be written up as a model of good practice and distributed to all English teachers within the authority. For the sake of the argument let us suppose these teachers are all employed by the same local education authority and that a central role is played by some powerful figure within that authority, say, the appropriate local authority adviser. The group has been called together on the initiative and under the auspices of this adviser. How will Doris cope in her early days? How is the evaluation to be accomplished? In fact Doris has a number of options open to her. For example, she could define the task as concerned with the specification and measurement of behavioural changes in the teachers, or alternatively in the pupils in their classes. Questions of any change in attitude on the part of the teachers could also present themselves. On the other hand, in order to assess the impact of the project, Doris might provide a series of case studies of those departments where the teachers work. The availability of resources may well constrain the actual choice(s) made. In this case both the funding agency and the adviser have agreed that the evaluation task is to provide a portrayal of the programme: its context and consequences.

At a very early stage in the process of accomplishing this task Doris meets several problems in which the exercise of personal skill is a concomitant of the research activity. For example, given the background and proposed audience of the teachers' thoughts, Doris begins to frame a hypothesis: namely, that who attends meetings and who does not (or who drops out) is a prospectively interesting question to be investigated. (In another context precisely this aspect is currently being explored in Jean Ruddock's evaluation of the effectiveness of short in-service courses being sponsored by the Schools Council.) The question interests Doris in terms of organization. For example, what support is needed for teachers engaged in this sort of out-of-school activity? What problems does a changing group membership pose for continuity? How are new members dealt with both socially and in terms of giving them access to the thinking of the group to date? In addition there is also a pedagogic interest. Are the leavers rejecting the particular definitions of English teaching being offered by the group? Are newcomers joining for the opposite reason? How much attitude change is actually going on (or is it the attitudes that remain and the people who change)? Whose views of English teaching hold sway? Is the group an agent of the authority?

At this particular point, at an early stage in the evaluation, these are no more than possibilities, questions raised by individual teachers during informal conversations before and after meetings, over a coffee or a game of billiards, or at other meetings not connected with the project activity. Doris now has to decide whether such questions should become formalized and incorporated into an evaluation strategy geared towards a portrayal of the project contexts and consequences. This requires formal access to at least one group of people – those who have left – that could be seen as having a more or less critical attitude towards the project activity. Unfortunately, efforts to accomplish this part of the evaluation task have an undesirable side-effect. Such an investigation is highly visible to powerful gatekeepers (in this case the local authority advisor). Questions asked, information sought, courtesy requests for access to non-participants soon begin to add up, to assume significance. It becomes clear that Doris is approaching what is to some a sensitive area of knowledge. Her questions are seen as a threat to the status quo.

Such sensitivity may well be heightened in the case of evaluation research as one consequence of the actual evaluation appointment. It is not untypical that evaluator researchers are chosen for their sympathy (if only as expressed at an interview) to whatever innovation is being tried out; sympathy, moreover, that may well have undergone a subtle period of testing of which the researcher was often unaware (Lyons, 1977). Such testing out is an acknowledged part of the research process (Hammond (1964), Castaneda (1968), Johnson (1975)). It is therefore almost taken as given that the approached group can be expected to be particularly sensitive to subtle (and not so subtle) changes in the definition of the activity. The suggestion here is not that Doris is engaged in some covert or highly secret strategy. It is rather a case of an issue emerging through casual conversation, interviews, etc.; of an initial glimmer becoming an idea. The importance of this occurring in the early days in the field, together with the necessary tentativeness of the whole idea at this stage, is perhaps significant.

However, *before* the idea is incorporated into the evaluation in any systematic way it becomes apparent that this view is not considered appropriate by the (powerful) local authority advisor. This view is expressed by jokes and pointed remarks, and gatekeepers who may try to guide research in particular directions are a well-known phenomenon (see, for example, Bogdan and Taylor, 1973). Social policy literature discusses this in terms of the relative powers for *implementation* of researchers and clients (Marris and Rein (1972)), although its implications for the activity of accomplishing evaluation research is not yet much discussed in the curriculum evaluation literature. In this case the advisor sees membership of the group as non-problematic. By raising it Doris is seen as disruptive and imposing a criterion that is not seen as relevant. Moreover, because of the sponsored nature of the evaluation research (in this case by the Schools Council), the approach is seen as overtly threatening. As Parlett and Hamilton (1972) suggest, such hostility towards Doris can be at least partially explained precisely because she is observing individuals at a critical time in their life (and project participants, including Doris, have their own career patterns). Many will have a high personal invest-ment in the activity. It is fundamentally disturbing to be observed and commented upon in this way. Indeed, this tension can be paralleled in the experience of the evaluator-researcher, one of whom has commented: 'the evaluator plays several roles. Wearing his "pure researcher" cap he may view certain happenings (which while wearing his "critical friend" cap were considered insignificant) as most valuable data'. In the light of this it is perhaps not so surprising that powerful gatekeepers of the approached group possess a tendency to view exposure of areas they see as threatening, or as not appropriate to the research activ-ity, as constituting some sort of professional foul.

This quotation is also of interest for the light it throws on a further structural tension, and one that is of more than passing relevance to Parsons's argument. This is the extent to which institutionalized training in a discipline may inculcate particular sensitivities and particular perspec-tives (or relatively natural ways to see the world). The difficulty is that the issue I am exploring at this point is not too frequently reported in the literature. In this context, and in the absence of documented instances, I find it dif-ficult to articulate the problems but would none the less like to flag a methodological agenda item that can perhaps be taken up on another occasion. The way in is probably the two complementary papers produced by Biott (1981) and myself (1978) in which we examine how much of a participant the researcher-participant-observer can become and still maintain a research stance. We were both working full-time in our respective institution(s) whilst researching into them. We both concluded that the experi-ence of doing research eventually effectively meant that we were no longer experiencing important (for us) aspects of institutional life as those who were not doing research experienced it. To an extent the necessary reflexivity of the research act made us outsiders on the inside. Our (disciplined) research base had made our relatively natural way of viewing the world essentially different from the view of the 'complete' participant. Put crudely this could be developed into an argument that the different training in different disciplines (for example, the difference between being an anthropologist or a statistician) may heighten this particular awareness to an extent that their ways of viewing the world are in fact relatively unnatural. For example, and very crudely, the initial response of the psychometrician would be to measure it; that of the ethnographer to describe it.

In the context of Doris accomplishing her evaluation, she was naturally drawn to the departmental case study cum programme portrayal rather than to measuring attitudes. The extent to which Doris, as a sociologist, was peculiarly sensitive towards the more covert and unintended aspects of the project activity remains a speculative question. How one's general perspective reveals itself professionally seems to be an extremely under-explored area in the accomplishment of evaluation. What I have tried to do in this brief aside is to set out my no more than intuitive feeling that Parsons is fundamentally mistaken in his *a priori* attempt to separate out the notion of personal skills from the mainstream of (discipline-based) procedural features in evaluation.

Evaluation accomplished

A reflexive methodology is not purely an exercise in social skills, nor is it some terribly introspective analysis (although this is always a danger), but a real and vital strand in the richly interactive tapestry of curriculum development. It would be important to acknowledge that the new wave evaluators are not alone in demanding a combination of personal and professional skills. Some personal qualities are required in most social research. For example, in order to achieve a satisfactory response rate, even (say) in the case of a random postal questionnaire, most researchers would acknowledge the need to accompany the questionnaire with a letter of explanation which seeks to enlist the respondents' support and co-operation. However, and particularly in the case of the new evaluation, the criteria by which socio-personal experiences become relevant to emerging theory must be made explicit. This can only be achieved by greater discussion based on cases teasing out important issues.

The work of Becker *et al*. (1961) and Johnson (1975) suggests that the period preceding and accompanying formal entry into the field can often be a time of personal and professional stress for the evaluator-researcher. Lyons (1977) offers a glimpse of the sorts of questions that will be constantly intruding into the evaluator-researcher's mind as she reflects upon the task – questions, moreover, the answers to which may prove quite consequential to the progress of the evaluation. For example, the beginning evaluator is faced with a potentially vast number of people and groupings whom she/he might approach. In the words of Lyons (1977):

> one of the first tasks of the evaluator . . . to decide where to begin. What was to be looked at? How was it to be looked at, and what viewpoint was to be adopted? Even these seemingly very straightforward questions were to prove problematic (p. 18).

The questions as much as the eventual answers may prove a considerable source of tension. Let us take the exemplar question, 'What was to be looked at and how?'

What to look at is itself a dimension involving the personal quality of the evaluator-researcher with which Parsons is so concerned. This is best illustrated by imagining a spectrum of activity represented at one extreme by a situa-
which there exists only a minimum requirement to
on personal qualities. Anyone would be able to

blunder about and yet collect the required information. Examples might include the colour scheme of a staff room, where people sit at a conference, or the collection of information about numbers of students on school rolls, going on to take 'A' levels etc. As with the random postal questionnaire some personal and social skill may be required in collecting this information. However, having said this, such skills do not significantly intrude into the research activity. In such cases it is the information that is sensitive, or not, as the case may be. In such cases the degree of personal skill that may be called for is related to the type of knowledge sought. Thus, whilst examples from this end of the spectrum would probably *tend* to adopt a statistical approach, this will not necessarily be the case since there are also sensitive boundaries in statistical research – for example, the collection of statistics relating to suicide (Douglas, 1970). As with the comparatively recent attempt by the Department of Education to collect information about numbers of immigrants in schools, or, more recently, details of how local education authorities go about organizing the school curricula, or the collection of 'A' level results in Manchester, high degrees of social skill may be involved. The personal and social skill on call is that of persuading people to let you be there, actually to collect the information. To this extent such skills are highly relevant to the research activity and, indeed, of some consequence for the content of any report.

However, there is another dimension of the evaluation research activity in which personal and social skills will impinge on the research in a far more direct manner. One of the non-sensitive cases referred to was the question of where people sit at a conference (or what have you). It is possible that the collection of this information is routine but that its interpretation – a matter of professional expertise – is highly controversial. The opposite case in such a continuum would be represented by those situations in which no amount of personal skill will avoid conflict. Here the situation is so sensitive that merely being there at all, or asking a particular question, will upset whatever delicate pattern of checks and balances is already in existence. Certainly those involved in the new wave evaluation are more likely to be found at this end of the spectrum, both because of its concern with the process of decision-making and because of the progressive nature of the illumination. In such a context a reflexive evaluation along the lines indicated by Gouldner can be expected to develop a greater awareness of sensitive boundaries: points beyond which the evaluation is not allowed to proceed, areas of taboo constraining the enquiry, questions not seen as legitimate by the different groups of respondents, and the relative accessibility of the different groups involved. The new wave evaluator-researchers can be expected to be especially sensitive in these respects. To this extent at least then it does matter that the methodological appendix is read, that the constraints and opportunities affecting the research process are revealed. Platt (1976), for example, is very illuminating in respect of methodological appendices as revealers of holes in the apparently seamless garment of the research.

Evaluation research is always in danger of becoming an essentially conservative activity and this is particularly so when experience becomes institutionalized because of an existing methodology. For example, Tipton (1977) notes the imbalance between the number of researches carried out into schools vis-à-vis other social institutions. Quite apart from whether or not this is true, there is certainly an apparent unwillingness for educational researches in general, and curriculum evaluation in particular, to draw upon insights generated on (say) the shop floor (Parsons, 1976). In an interesting way this imbalance parallels those critiques of school curricula emanating from industrialists and trade unionists. Moreover, even accepting this limitation, researches of the school suffer a serious deficiency. Dale (1972) comments that there are many studies of the classroom, yet relatively few of school staffrooms, the head teacher's study, or indeed the Schools Council. Such areas of study might be expected to be sensitive and highlight some of the constraints under which evaluation is accomplished.

Framing a methodology

The world of the evaluator-researcher is argued to be an active accomplishment. Indeed, a characteristic of such research is that it draws attention to the strategic decisions made throughout the period of research and one of the anticipated outcomes of this paper is that this argument will be placed on the agenda for public discussion in the evaluation research literature. The following section thus aims to provide at least one conceptual framework within which personal qualities can be legitimately discussed as part of the professional expertise of the evaluation community.

Those evaluator-researchers approaching dilemmas such as that confronting Doris will be approaching what is acknowledged to be a critical event in the progress of the evaluation that will probably call upon any reserves in their personal qualities. None the less, having said this, it has been argued that such events will likely not be just about personal skills (if they ever were) but about how the people involved define their situation. The focus of this paper is the interaction between personal qualities and professional skills and this is conceptualized in the illustration on page 106. Whilst it is probably empirically correct that most existing evaluation research – at least in the sense of reports that are publicly available – occurs in area A (quantitative research requiring little recourse to social skill) and area D (qualitative research involving a high degree of social skill), this need not necessarily be the case. None the less, most existing evaluation research does occur along the A–D axis (and the existence of this

	Public, non-sensitive knowledge	Private, sensitive knowledge
A predominantly quantitative methodology	A	B
A predominantly qualitative methodology	C	D

phenomenon may itself be a cause for concern). Nor, indeed, is this bias necessary. For example, if one takes recent interest in establishing the extent of reportable physical punishment in schools, then this is on the face of it quantitative empirical research of a high order. However, the issue is at present sufficiently sensitive for it also to demand a high order of social skill. Such exercises would, on this model, appear in area B.

It is with area C that there is some difficulty in providing appropriate examples. Perhaps the complete (hidden) observer (Junker, 1960) or the complete participant would be the nearest approximation to an evaluation research methodology carried out in this context. Certainly evaluation research carried out by the Schools Council has made insufficient acknowledgement of the contribution to be made by inside research (Woods (1977), Smetherham (1978)). At this moment the work of the Ford Teaching Project is perhaps the nearest evaluation equivalent. Indeed, since much sponsored research is concentrated and this sort of exercise is a relatively long-term activity, it may be that the construction of the evaluation research activity as conceived by the Schools Council prevents this. It would also need to be acknowledged that apparently similar incidents can constitute different events and be differently interpreted at different points in the evaluation as relationships and their meanings undergo subtle changes. For example, the literature is full of references to grounded theory (Glaser and Strauss, 1968) and to progressive focusing (Pocklington and Jamieson, 1976), yet there is little discussion of the social and methodological consequences that accompany the implied sharpening up of the enquiry. Unfortunately, this specific aspect of the general problem of reactivity (although the *modus operandi* of the evaluator-researcher) is not well documented. This despite the fact that many of the questions with which any fieldworker must come to terms are heightened in curriculum evaluation. The pity is that in both cases the process has tended to remain hidden from public gaze. In educational research, it is still a rarity to find that the teachers' and perhaps the pupils' *reaction* to a research report have been followed up as an integral part of the research. If correct this is a very suggestive line of enquiry and directs attention to a major concern of this paper in providing a methodological rationale for the evaluation activity. The point is that, in evaluation as in any kind of research, the evaluator is engaged in a process of building up knowledge in which various difficulties latent in any research assume a greater significance in curriculum evaluation. In particular, not only the questions asked direct attention to their content, but also the early testing out of hypotheses, triangulations, etc. all become incremental and part of the action.

Since the model is interactive and the knowledge both of and about the evaluator *vis-à-vis* the approached groups is incremental, the areas are not fixed designations. However, the model does tease out the points at which questions of ethics, of the conflicting commitments of the researcher, would begin to assert themselves. The question avoided in this paper is, having gained confidences (although not necessarily confidential information) what happens next? The desired effect of these examples is to counsel against any attempt to plot particular studies at a particular and definitive point on the model. What is being considered is rather a general area for the purpose of analysis. According to the particular methodology and direction of the research, the area might skew off in whatever direction is indicated. Moreover, the model is essentially multi-dimensional: for example, it does not explicitly allow for the incremental nature of knowledge built up along *both* dimensions. Similarly, it only implicitly acknowledges the relative powers of the various participants to control another's access to information.

Conclusion

Hamilton *et al.* (1977) argue, in an editorial introduction to the section on alternative methodology, that:

> What is an unacceptable invasion of privacy in one investigation is a probing, useful and popular analysis in another. What is a totally unwarranted abuse of evaluative privilege in one instance is a highly acceptable and necessary intervention in another. (p. 168)

Unfortunately, this comment invokes a criterion for judging such situations that has yet to be made explicit. In what circumstances does a particular case constitute a probing analysis rather than an unacceptable invasion of privacy? In what circumstances can similar actions be described as an abuse of privilege on the one hand, and as a highly acceptable and necessary intervention on the other?

Without knowing the context or the criteria, the answer is that we cannot tell. The evidence does not exist. Parsons (1980) is right to be concerned at an evaluation research methodology dominated by the exercise of 'personal quality'. However, there may be occasions when the exercise of personal quality is a concomitant of the research act; indeed, that there is an established research paradigm within which such a perspective can be incorporated. Doris has been used as one example demonstrating the potential usefulness of an eclectic evaluation research methodology once such accounts become public. 'Personal skills' cannot be justifiably divorced from the situational context of evaluation. Although in commonsense terms we often speak of personal skills as though they were entirely non-situational, even the Armed Forces now seem to have abandoned the Etonian notion of 'leadership' as something that one carries around ready to apply like a social poultice to any situation where people seem not to know what they are doing. The optimistic breakaway in illuminative evaluation for me is in the possibilities for rigour of *procedures*, and I would tend to see 'personal skills' as a category of that rigour.

What I am asking for are tighter procedural hypotheses – more evidence about what happens when certain procedures are adopted or overlooked, in terms of good or bad facilitative relationships between evaluator and client. These are of course highly situational factors and the more evaluators can provide accounts of their work and their reflections on the problems encountered, the more will this facilitate discussion and identification of the common issues. In this way evidence can be made available to help frame a coherent evaluation methodology particularly for the guidance of new researchers working in the field. Then evaluators can begin to build personal codes of practice which, even if constantly found wanting, will nevertheless provide a better basis for situational judgement than presently exists in the craft. Theory in education can only be tested through access; and access may call for procedural development. A 'deep structures' position in the disciplinary sense may well be a feature of these procedures.

In this paper, as in life, Doris has been left confronting an appalling dilemma. Will she drop this promising line of investigation or will she confront the situation, thereby risking unpleasantness and a possible closing down of the research? In fact, and in an interesting way, Doris represents precisely the type of problem indicated by Tipton

(1977) in her discussion on the tense relationship existing between (in her case) sociology and educational administration. The difficulty is that, at present, there is no shared language for discussing the problem. The tentative model suggested in his paper represents one attempt to legitimize such accounts, thereby enabling a body of evaluation (method) literature to be built up and eventually leading to the establishment of a coherent evaluation methodology, a public epistemology that develops from a continuous and incremental reflection about the problems encountered during the conduct of particular studies.

References

Atkinson, P. (1978) *Research Methods in Education and the Social Sciences: Research Design*. DRAFT, DE304, Block 3, Part 5. Milton Keynes: Open University Press.

Becher, T. (1978) The shackles fall. Review of Hamilton *et al*. (1977) in *The Times Educational Supplement*, 10 February 1978, 23.

Becker, H. S. (1967) Whose side are we on? *Social Problems* **14**, 239–47.

——, Geer, B., Hughes, E.C. & Strauss, A. (1961) *Boys in White, Student Culture in Medical School*. University of Chicago Press.

Bell, C. & Newby, H. (eds.) (1977) *Doing Sociological Research*. London: Allen & Unwin.

Berger, P. L. & Luckmann, T. (1967) *The Social Construction of Reality*. Harmondsworth: Penguin.

Biott, C. (1981) Evaluator, Researcher, Participant. In D. Smetherham *Practising Evaluation*. Driffield, Yorkshire: Nafferton Books.

Bogdan, R. & Taylor, S. J. (1973) *Introduction to Qualitative Research Methods*. New York: Wiley.

Bolam, R., Smith, G. & Canter, H. (1978) Research report:

local education authority and educational innovation. In *Educational Administration* **6**, 19–31.

Castaneda, C. (1968) *The Teachings of Don Juan*. Harmondsworth: Penguin.

Dale, R. (1972) *The Culture of the School*. Milton Keynes: Open University Press.

Dalton, M. (1959) *Men Who Manage*. New York: John Wiley.

Delamont, S. (1968) *Sociology and the Classroom in Sociological Interpretations of Schooling and Classrooms*. Driffield, Yorkshire: Nafferton Books.

Deutscher, I. (1973) *What We Say/What We Do: Sentiments and Acts*. Glenview, Ill.: Scott Foresman.

Douglas, J. D. (1970) *The Social Meanings of Suicide*. Princetown University Press.

Douglas, M. (1975) *Implicit Meanings*. London: Routledge & Kegan Paul.

Elliott, J. (1977) Conceptualising relationships between research/evaluation procedures and in-service teacher education. *British Journal of In-service Education* **3** (1), 102–14.

Glaser, B. & Strauss, A. (1968) *The Discovery of Grounded Theory*. New York: Aldine.

Goffman, E. (1971) *The Presentation of the Self in Everyday Life*. Harmondsworth: Penguin.

Gouldner, A. W. (1972) *The Coming Crisis of Western Sociology*. London: Heinemann.

Hamilton, D., Jenkins, D., King, C., MacDonald, B. & Parlett, M. (eds.) (1977) *Beyond the Numbers Game*. Basingstoke and London: Macmillan.

Hammond, P. E. (1964) *Sociologists at Work*. London: Basic Books.

Hargreaves, D. (1968) *Social Relations in a Secondary School*. London: Routledge & Kegan Paul.

Harre, R. & Secord, P. F. (1972) *The Explanation of Social Behaviour*. Oxford: Blackwell.

Johnson, J. M. (1975) *Doing Field Research*. London: Collier-Macmillan.

Junker, B. H. (1960) *Fieldwork: An Introduction to the Social Sciences*. University of Chicago Press.

Kelly, G. (1955) *The Psychology of Personal Constructs*. New York: Norton.

Lacey, C. (1976) Problems of sociological fieldwork, a review of the methodology of 'Hightown Grammar'. In Shipman (1976), 63–88.

Lyons, H. (1977) Evaluating a local curriculum development project. *Insight*, November.

Marris, P. & Rein, M. (1972) *Dilemmas of Social Reform*. London: Routledge & Kegan Paul.

Parlett, M. & Hamilton, D. (1972) *Evaluation as Illumination; a New Approach to the Study of Innovatory Programmes*. Occasional Paper 9, Centre for Research in the Educational Sciences, University of Edinburgh.

Parsons, C. (1976) The new evaluation. *Journal of Curriculum Studies* **8**(2).

—— (1980) Whither evaluation? A seminal paper presented for discussion at the University of London, Institute of Education/Schools Council series on curriculum evaluation.

Platt, J. (1976) *Realities of Social Research*. Edinburgh: Sussex University Press.

Pocklington, K. & Jamieson, M. (1976) An evolving research design in a study of educational provision for blind and partially sighted children. Paper presented to second annual conference, British Educational Research Association.

Shipman, M.D. (1976) *The Organisation and Impact of Social Research*. London: Routledge & Kegan Paul.

Shipman, M. D. with Bolam, D. & Jenkins, D. (1974) *Inside a Curriculum Project*. London: Methuen.

Shotter, J. (1975) *Images of Man in Psychological Research*. London: Methuen.

Simon, B. (1978) Educational research which way? *Research Intelligence* **4**, 2–7.

Smetherham, D. (1978) Insider research. *British Educa-*

tional Research Journal **4**(2), 97–102.

Tipton, B. (1977) The tense relationship of sociology and educational administration. *Educational Administration* **5**(2), 46–57.

Webb, E. J. (1966) *Unobtrusive Measures: Nonreactive Research in the Social Sciences*. Chicago: Rand McNally.

Wilson, S. (1977) Centre for new schools. Ethnographic techniques in educational research. In Hamilton *et al.* (1977), 193–200.

Woods, P. (1977) Stages in interpretive research. *Research Intelligence* **3**(1), 17–18.

5 Process evaluation in schools*

Helen Simons

In the current accountability debate process models of evaluation have been advanced as alternatives to accountability models that are based on product efficiency criteria (MacDonald (1978), Elliott (1978a)). In order to provide an appropriate model of accountability, it is argued, evaluation should aspire to reflect the processes of teaching, learning and schooling. We need to know not so much what pupils can be demonstrated to have learned (the focus of product models) but rather what transpires in the process of learning and teaching, the outcomes we could reasonably expect from such transactions and the strengths and weaknesses of educational provision. We need, in other words, to educate our judgements about the

*This paper was first presented at the Joint Seminar between the Schools Council Research team and the University of London Institute of Education Curriculum Studies Department, July 1978.

I wish to acknowledge my thanks to the numerous teachers who have discussed and tested the feasibility of the proposals outlined here over the past two years, and especially to two generations of MA students in the Department of Curriculum Studies, University of London Institute of Education. I also wish to thank the members of the Joint Seminar for their helpful comments on the presentation of this paper and Colin Lacey for his constructive editorial guidance and support in the preparation of this paper for this publication.

adequacy of provision for learning and the quality of experience pupils have.

One of the best ways to improve these judgements is to study the processes of teaching, learning and schooling in order to be able to compare practice with intention, opportunities with aspirations. And one of the best ways to represent and promote understanding of these processes is to accumulate and make available detailed descriptions of teaching and learning and the values and effects of curriculum policies within the context of particular schools and classrooms. Such an approach could take into account actual as well as intended practice and indicate the range of ways achievements might be demonstrated.

Product models emphasize measurable learnings, teaching intentions, and how efficiently the intentions have been achieved. The concept is an economic one and fits best within a system where resources can be allocated and assessed directly in relation to outputs by measures such as achievement tests. Such an approach has an appealing logic, but its defence rests upon a dangerous oversimplification of education and evaluation.

The worth of educational experience, as Stake (1978) has pointed out, can rarely be demonstrated by such measures:

> The worth of a program is seldom indicated by the achievement of students. That is partly true because our measurement instruments are narrow and crude. They indicate only a small part of the impact of a lesson or a program. (We should continue to refine and redesign our objective measures of attainment, but we should not design evaluation studies now as if satisfactory instruments existed.) It is also partly true because the worth of a program is dependent on its relevance to other courses and programs, on its effect on teacher morale, on its compatibility with community ideology, etc.

The adequacy of the product efficiency model for educational purposes is often not questioned before it is invoked. And it is often invoked when questions are being asked about the value of money spent or when a society, or groups in society, wish to stress specific outcomes for instrumental purposes. Testing programmes based on this model, some argue, are a most powerful instrument of curriculum control and social engineering. (See, for example, House, 1973a.) The multi-purpose nature of education and backwash effects of such schemes are overlooked in the adoption of product-efficiency models. It is partly to redress this imbalance (but also for other reasons associated with the deficiencies of such approaches discussed below) that process evaluation is now being strongly advocated by some educationalists.

This paper presents a case for process evaluation in the context of evaluating the whole school. Process, as already indicated, can refer to the teaching/learning interface and several authors have written extensively about the need for evaluation of these processes. (See, for example, Elliott (1978b), Stenhouse (1975).) Others refer to the whole process of schooling (MacDonald (1978), Simons (1978)). Both kinds of evaluation have been suggested as alternatives to current accountability models. Both have been closely linked to self-evaluation, thereby challenging the political as well as the content assumptions of orthodox thinking.

These evaluations can take different forms. The particular stance towards school self-evaluation advanced here is one which encourages a high degree of participation in the conduct of the evaluation and the sharing of knowledge.

Three main arguments are presented. First it is argued that the major justification for school self-evaluation is enhanced professionalism and that it is best introduced as a continuing part of professional practice, not as a short-term response to political pressures. Secondly, it is suggested that, in the short term, development of the process model needs to be insulated from accountability demands.

Thirdly, and in the long term, it argues that such evaluation will provide a more effective and constructive model of accountability than many of the current models in use. Drawing on the initial experience of a group who undertook a school self-evaluation, some of the problems and potential of this approach in practice are then discussed.

One of the springboards for the surge of interest in school self-evaluation over the past five years has been reaction to the setting up of the Assessment of Performance Unit (APU) by central government. Doubts have been cast on the capacity of the APU testing programme to provide an adequate picture of the achievements of our schools (MacDonald (1978), Harlen (1979b)), and concerns have been expressed about the constraints such a centralized monitoring programme might impose on the curriculum. The dangers associated with externally imposed schemes have been highlighted to encourage schools to respond by undertaking their own school evaluations, producing evidence of the quality and worth of what they are doing in ways determined by them.

Whilst encouraging such initiatives myself, I have also argued (Simons, 1980) that the most important justification for undertaking school self-evaluation is to enhance the professional image and practice of teachers and schools. The current accountability climate may provide a context and impetus for the development of forms of evaluation but not a stable underpinning. Schools may be tempted to respond to externally imposed schemes by producing whatever is required without themselves using the data for review of the professional practice of the school. Even if the activity does affect practice in positive ways, it may cease when the external demand fades.

If schools initiate evaluations in response to their own needs (and these may include producing accounts for outside audiences) these efforts are likely to be more sustained, to reflect the actual experience of schools and to lead to a quality control which is in the hands of those who have the prime responsibility for educating children and running the schools. It is primarily for these reasons that I wish to emphasize that the most appropriate justification for school self-evaluation is educational and professional and to suggest that it should be established as an integral part of professional practice.

Now that the era of national curriculum development projects seems to be over, the time is especially right for schools to evaluate themselves. Over the past two decades evaluation has become a highly specialized activity – the end of a chain of central development and diffusion invoked to see whether such central investment has been worthwhile. It has generally been costly, technical and specialized. Results and learnings from project evaluations have not been easy to apply to the varying circumstances of individual schools and classrooms.

What I am suggesting here is:

1   that the sequence be reversed – evaluation should precede curriculum development and not follow in its wake;

2   that the style of evaluation more closely reflect the ways in which schools do evaluate the quality of education they provide;

3   that the evaluation be undertaken and managed by the schools themselves;

4   that the evaluation focus on intra-institutional issues.

In making these suggestions I do not imply that little evaluation currently takes place in schools. Heads, teachers and pupils are continuously making judgements about teaching, the curriculum and the school. Policies are changed and decisions made implicitly drawing upon these judgements. But such evaluations are informal, frequently non-systematic and private to individuals or groups within the school: they are not part of a shared, co-ordinated and public tradition.

In the current climate pressure is being put upon schools by parents, politicians and employers to demonstrate their worth. But many of the indices being sought focus solely on pupil outcomes. These are only one measure of the worth of a school. Much more needs to be evaluated including curriculum policies, learning opportunities, the interrelationships between levels (pupil, classroom, school) and forms of provision and achievements. The specific case for such a broader evaluation is outlined below. The emphasis is on evaluation of the school as a whole, or a policy issue which concerns the whole school. Information on pupil achievement or teacher performance may form part of the evaluation if it is relevant to the issue chosen for study, but is not focused upon directly. (For a discussion of the evaluation of pupil learning and teacher performance, see, respectively, Harlen (1978, 1979a), and Elliott (1978b, 1979).)

The case for school self-evaluation

The case for studying the school as a whole is based on the following assumptions:

1 that better understanding of the organization and policies of the school could improve the opportunities and experiences provided in classrooms;

2 that systematic study and review allows the school to determine, and to produce evidence of, the extent to which they are providing the quality of education they espouse;

3 that a study of school policies can help teachers identify policy effects which require attention at school, department or classroom level;

4 that many policy issues (remedial education, for example), cut across departments and classrooms and require collective review and resolution;

5 that there are many learning experiences (fieldwork

and extra-curricular activities, for instance) which do not take place in the classroom and which require the co-operation and appraisal of the whole school;

6 that participation in a school self-study gives teachers the opportunity to develop their professional decision-making skills, enlarge their perspectives, and become better informed about the roles, responsibilities and problems of their colleagues.

Description of process evaluation

It is perhaps important before proceeding further to describe some of the characteristics of school process self-evaluation. What distinguishes it from other forms of evaluation? In what ways can it contribute to our understanding of education.

Studies of the process of learning and schooling will tend to be descriptive/analytic, particular, small scale. They will record events in progress, document observations and draw on the judgements and perspectives of participants in the process – teachers, pupils, heads – in coming to understand observations and events in a specific context. Close description both of practice and the social context is an important part of the study. Such descriptions provide opportunities for interpretations that elude other models of assessment or evaluation based on assumptions of comparability and elimination of variation. Such descriptions also provide opportunities for more of the complexity of educational experience to be grasped and articulated.

While the process could start with an examination of information that already exists in the school (see p.124), process evaluation differs from reports to school governors, information given to parents, or the school prospectus in going beyond the information given to examining the assumptions and values underlying this information. Descriptions of practice, examples of outcomes, observations and analysis of different perspectives on issues may all form part of the process.

Reports to governors and parents are changing in many schools with the giving of more detailed information, and that provides, of course, a basis for outside evaluation to begin to take place. The evaluation process described here emphasizes that evaluation should start within the school in a context of informing the school's policy-making and improving educational practice. Reports with this aspiration are likely to be more interpretative than factual, to focus on particular policy issues, to expose different value positions, to provide evidence for decision-making and to raise options or alternatives for action.

Subjective judgements are an important part of the process. This needs to be emphasized, so undervalued are such judgements in many approaches to educational research and evaluation. Professional judgements are an integral part of classroom transactions and policy decisions. The subtlety of judgement may be difficult to capture but in evaluating the process of teaching, learning and schooling, the judgements of people are an important source of data it would be foolish to ignore if understanding of the complexity of these processes is sought. There are difficulties, of course, in relying solely on judgement or, rather, on any one person's judgement, but in an evaluation utilizing a range of different methods and different people as sources, cross-checks on the accuracy of information can be established and the validity of judgements assessed.

While the focus may be particular, the data base is broad and may include quantitative and qualitative indicators of progress or events; and evidence of the outcomes as well as the processes of teaching, learning and schooling. Both may be needed, if relevant to the issue under review. But what is also important here, whatever kind of data is selected, is that it be considered within the context of the particular school. The point has often been made (but is nevertheless worth stressing again) that our understanding of schooling is likely to be more complete if we try and capture more of the detail of what actually transpires in classrooms and schools, and more accurate if we interpret findings in context, be they examination results, achievement scores, qualitative judgements or observations.

Cronbach (1975) has made the point before:

Instead of making generalization the ruling consideration in our research, I suggest that we reverse our priorities. An observer collecting data in one particular situation is in a position to appraise a practice or proposition in that setting, observing effects in context. In trying to describe and account for what happened, he will give equally careful attention to uncontrolled conditions, to personal characteristics and to events that occurred during treatment and measurement. As he goes from situation to situation, his first task is to describe and interpret the effect anew in each locale, perhaps taking into account factors that were unique to that locale or series of events. (Cf. Geertz, 1973, Chapter 1, on 'thick description'.)

It is also important to stress here that process approaches to evaluation (emphasizing description and interpretation, dynamics and context) do not reject quantitative data or suggest that, in paying more attention to the process, outcomes be neglected. (See, for example, Stake (1967), Parlett and Hamilton (1972).) The case for process evaluation and more qualitative observations has sometimes been overstated, I believe, as a reaction against the narrowness of product evaluations. The strength of the advocacy is also in direct proportion to the degree to which mechanistic models are being adopted compared with more qualitative approaches. Like any different approach the case may need to be overstated to be noticed at all. But it should not be taken to entail a neglect of outcomes. Indeed, it is likely that part of the evidence for evaluating the processes of learning and schooling will be outcome data. But there are many outcomes of schooling (qualitative and quantitative), and these need to be related to the aims of teaching, the opportunities provided for learning and to the transactions which occurred in the classroom and school. The objection to product-efficiency criteria measures is to the narrowness of the measure, and the use that is frequently made of such measures.

The provision of relevant information is a third characteristic. Part of the argument against existing models of accountability rest on the fact that they do not, as Stake has pointed out, provide *relevant* information on the *quality* of educational practice and provision (Stake, 1976). Descriptions of classroom practice and the ways in which policies are determined and translated within particular school contexts are likely to yield more relevant information for local decision-making, particularly if they utilize a range of information and judgements in describing and analysing the values, implicit or explicit, in the policies and practice. An understanding of different attitudes and values towards the policy issue under discussion is essential if modification or a change in policy is to be an outcome of the evaluation. It need not be, of course. Evaluation is undertaken initially for the purpose of reviewing current practice and coming to understand some of the strengths and weaknesses in present provision. Change is a possible outcome but a next stage decision. The decision may be to leave things as they are. If the decision is to change, it is hoped that the evaluation would have provided insights or leads as to how this might be done.

The question is sometimes raised as to the relevance of specific studies of schools for national accountability. They may not be relevant, except indirectly, and not in the short term. But that does not detract from their value. In a decentralized system where many of the decisions are in the hands of local authorities and schools, development of forms of evaluation appropriate to the schools and local settings is needed. Locally is where many of the decisions affecting the *quality* of provision are made.

A fourth characteristic is the utilization of information and skills already available. Much information which can form a data base for analysis already exists in the school. It includes, for example, information on examination results, the academic and pastoral structure, the option system, the qualifications and allocation of staff to subjects, the resources available and their allocation to departments. A more extensive list is offered by Mac-Donald (1978) in outlining the first of a three-stage process of school self-evaluation. Implicit in such information are questions of value. Even a brief analysis will provide a basis for the elucidation of policies, priorities and assumptions.

Where evaluation of a policy issue is sought for the explicit purpose of review, additional data may have to be collected. Useful methods which need not take a lot of time and which utilize skills teachers already have include questioning, listening, observation, and the noting of critical incidents and dialogue between different members of the school. Data collected in these ways does not in itself, however, provide evidence – it has to be related to the issues and cross-checked for accuracy. Similarly, data will not provide information to help decision-making unless the issues are presented in a form that is easily assimilated, a mechanism exists for the discussion of such evaluation, and a commitment is undertaken by the whole school to considering the evaluation as a basis for decision-making. Written reports are economical and the most usual way of presenting information. But if they are to be used as a basis for discussion they need to be evocative rather than prescriptive, i.e. to raise questions, options, alternatives. Reports which are closed – tendentious, argumentative or conclusive – are rarely helpful for collective decision making purposes. Written reports can, of course, be supplemented by recordings, examples of pupils' work, photographs. But in general these take more time both to produce and assimilate.

How any particular school sets up the appropriate procedures to evaluate the policy issue chosen and to utilize
the evaluation to inform decision-making can only be
determined in the particular context of each school in
relation to the time available, the personnel who will
undertake the evaluation and the ethos of the school, but
some general principles necessary to ensure that the
evaluation has a reasonable chance of being taken seriously and is instituted as part of a continuing process are
indicated in a related paper (Simons, 1980).

My second argument – that in the short term school
self-evaluation needs to be separated from accountability
demands – is adopted for several reasons. The first concerns
the nature of the exercise itself. Opening one's policies and
practices to critique in a system characterized by privacy
for so long can be a challenging but threatening exercise.
What was once implicit now becomes explicit. What was
once informal or the province of one or two staff now
becomes an accepted part of the school's agenda for study.
Even the most commonplace events and policy statements
can raise controversy when the assumptions underlying
such events and statements are discussed.

It is also the case, of course, that maintaining fictions
about practice or the institution may be functional in
preserving its stability, and this is a stability that many
may not want to see disturbed – at least without some
control over how and to what extent. For this reason I
have, elsewhere, (Simons, 1978) suggested a set of principles and procedures which give participants some control
over the process and some protection from the risks of
self-evaluation while they gain experience in document-
ing their own work.

Secondly, it seems important that school self-evaluation
be protected for a time from public scrutiny to allow
schools to build up the necessary evaluation skills to produce self-accounts. Some evidence for this point of view is
presented in the final section of this paper. The ability of

teachers to engage in this activity is not in doubt. One of the major premises on which school self-evaluation is based is that teachers and schools are self-evaluating all the time and already possess the skills and the knowledge to describe and analyse their policies and practices in a relevant context. It is, however, not common practice at the moment (although the trend is growing) and a certain amount of time is needed for schools to produce self-accounts and for teachers and outsiders to become familiar with the kind of data which is offered and the criteria by which self-accounts should be valued.

Given this situation it would be unfair at the present time to use a school self-evaluation as a school audit. Reflecting on one's practice can be disturbing in itself as those who have been through the process testify. Support is needed to sustain the exercise. Honest accounts of one's practice could be construed as evidence of weakness and possibly used as a basis for alleging incompetence. With so many highly qualified teachers on the market, it is not inconceivable that some heads and LEAs might want to use self-evaluation for this purpose.

A third reason, not unconnected with the second, is the use to which these accounts may be put. Pressures to go public too soon, particularly in a context of threatened closure of schools and teacher unemployment, may simply result in window-dressing or positive, glowing accounts. After all, what school is going to open itself to critique if that critique, undertaken in a genuine spirit of self-examination, has any chance of being used to arm its critics or put individuals at risk? Given the changing nature of governance and management of schools and the increasing interest by parents and employers about what goes on in schools such an outcome is a possibility. One hopes, of course, that LEAs would not put the schools in such a position should they decide to undertake school self-evaluation; that they would respect their need for time to experiment with the process and production of

such accounts and not expect to use them as an accountability mechanism before an appropriate time.

There seems little doubt that LEAs are increasing their
interest in gaining more information about schools; some
by taking up the DES's initiative to undertake parallel
local testing to APU testing, others by strengthening the
nature of the adviser's role to include an assessment or
evaluation component. In several authorities LEAs have
changed the name of their advisers to inspectors in preparation for the role they, or the elected members, think
advisers should assume. Some advisers have undertaken
their own surveys of schools. In one authority where this
occurred, while objecting to the intrusion teachers
nevertheless recognized that advisers were also under pressure to justify their existence. That LEAs should have more
information about schools is not at issue. What may be at
issue is the kind of information sought, the means by
which it is gathered and the purpose for which it is used.
Ideally, schools and LEAs would have a consistent and
mutual agreement on the position to be taken with regard
to each of these questions.

A fourth related reason which is the core of the main
argument concerns the structure of the educational system. Given the way the system is structured at present,
more information about schools means more information
in the hands of those who have the power to control
resources: the DES gets more information about schools;
the LEAs get more information about schools; the heads
get more information about their staff and pupils. Those in
a hierarchical, and usually more powerful position, in
short, get more information about those who are less powerful in the system. What is more, they may use their
power, as already implied, to get access to evaluations
undertaken by other sectors of the service for one purpose
(e.g. self-reflection of schools policies and practice) and
use these for another purpose (e.g. resource allocation,
employment decisions). If schools are to be more open to

public scrutiny and be called to account for how they carry out their responsibilities, it does not seem unreasonable to suggest that the other sectors of the education service do the same. Information flows one way at present – upwards.

The introduction of the APU monitoring does little to counteract this view if House (1973a) is right about the control assumptions underlying the hierarchical nature of most accountability schemes.

> In most schemes the goals are formulated by the higher levels of authority so that accountability becomes a strongly hierarchic matter. Teachers formulate goals for students, administrators for teachers, school boards for administrators, etc. Even where goals are formulated by lower levels, the accountability data are reported to those above. Students report to teachers, teachers to administrators, local agencies to state agencies, etc. Education is organized like a gigantic corporation in which each subordinate is strictly accountable to his boss. Few schemes suggest that the teacher be accountable to the student, to the parent, to his peers, or even to his own conscience. In essence, the individual is accountable to the institution, but the institution is not accountable to the individual.

Local authority accountability schemes which propose to follow the APU testing initiative are based on similar assumptions, but have an even more dangerous potential effect. Since LEAs have more direct control over resource allocation in the local environment, teacher employment and promotion, it is possible that the results could be used not simply to establish the state of overall pupil achievement but for decision-making. Those LEAs which have indicated their intention to undertake testing parallel to APU testing have also announced their intention to test all schools and not adopt the plan of light sampling adopted by the APU. Schools could be identifiable and resource decisions made in response to test achievements. Local authorities which choose to test are being offered assistance in this process by the setting up of the item bank project for local authorities at the NFER funded by the DES.

The point raised by House has a further implication in the context of encouraging schools to produce self-accounts. It concerns the openness and flow of information. How fair is it in the current climate to encourage schools to produce self-accounts detailing their practice and school policies, the grounds on which decisions are taken and the achievements reached, if other institutions to which they report are not to do the same? It would seem reasonable to expect that if schools are being asked to produce self-accounts of their practice and achievements, other sectors of the service should do likewise. In a democratic society the principles of openness and sharing of knowledge cannot be confined to particular groups.

It is perhaps important to point out here that in suggesting that schools control the availability of self-reports to outside audiences, I am not advocating that they become less open to public scrutiny. Quite the contrary. The issue is one of timing, confidence and credibility. I believe teachers and schools should be accountable and report upon the work of the school to parents and the community. But in order to demonstrate accountability they must be given autonomy. External imposition of accountability schemes may not produce a self-reflective teaching profession but simply engender defensiveness and hostility. This is partly because of the nature of external schemes – which emphasize measurable outcomes to the exclusion of other criteria – and partly because of the imposition itself. The most effective way of ensuring accountability is not to restrict people's autonomy but to make them accountable for it.

Giving control to schools over the timing of release of self-accounts is compatible with the concept of autonomy and is necessary for the reasons stated on pages 125–6 concerning the production and criteria of self-accounts. The argument is not one for greater secrecy on the part of schools but for quality control as the first stage in a process of gradually making information more accessible.

The third argument of this paper is that a process model of school self-evaluation can provide a more positive form of accountability than the current models in use. The dominant mode of accountability, House argues (1973a), is mechanistic, having 'productivity' as its ethic and power rather than professionalism at its core: 'Most accountability schemes – whether they be performance contracting, cost-benefit analysis, performance-based teacher education or whatever – apply a mechanical solution, a power solution, to reform complex social organizations.' They are often, he goes on to say, punishing on individuals – who fail to achieve the pre-specified outcomes – and distorting of reality, since a single measure of output of precisely defined objectives is often the only indicator of value.

Evaluation on process lines allows schools to demonstrate and to account for what they can reasonably be held to be accountable for, i.e. creating the opportunities for children to learn and for the quality of provision. Given the wide range of factors affecting pupil learning (home influence, social factors, individual differences, interest and motivation, relationships between pupils and teachers), in the last analysis teachers cannot be held to be entirely accountable for what pupils actually learn or fail to learn. There is no accounting for the fact that some children may choose not to learn or not to tell what they have learned. The indicators of learning that are often used in accountability schemes are also limited, if not simplistic: they reveal what pupils did learn or did not learn on one measure but fail to indicate pupil achievement on other dimensions of learning. They also fail to indicate what contributed or did not contribute to the learning.

Pupil achievement, in short, is too narrow a dimension

on which to base the case for accountability. Accountability should be related to responsibility and autonomy. Teachers should be held accountable not for the precise learning gains of pupils but for providing the appropriate opportunities for children to learn and for demonstrating the ways in which they have learned. Similarly, the LEAs should be held accountable for the adequacy of education provision and for justifying their spending priorities. The DES likewise should be held accountable for national provision, policy priorities and administration. All sectors of the service, in other words, should be accountable for those parts of the service they are responsible for and over which they have autonomy of decision-making.

When one considers the weight of educational evidence against accountability schemes based on mechanistic models, and America provides us with lots of examples (see, for instance, Read in House, 1973b, and House, 1979), it seems surprising that in England at the present time a testing programme is being mounted by the DES with the same in-built assumptions that have dominated the American testing movement for years and which have increasingly been challenged by leading American educationalists, including those strongly associated with the test industry in the past (Cronbach, 1975). One is tempted to conclude that the exercise is only a political response to anxiety over standards and that those in power find a technocratic, rather than an educational, approach towards assessing achievement more useful in placating their own critics.

But that may be unfair. It is hard to disagree with the aspiration of central government to monitor national standards of performance. What one can disagree with, and what is at issue here, is the mode of assessment adopted to reflect standards, the specific measurement models used and the backlash effects wide-scale testing may have on the curriculum. Particular difficulties with the Rasch model of item banking adopted by the NFER for mathematics and language teaching have been well articulated elsewhere (Goldstein and Blinkhorn (1977), Goldstein (1979)ꞌ). The constraining effects on the curriculum are reflected in the American 'back to basics' movement. Even if teachers do not teach to the test, those subjects or areas in the curriculum that are not tested may become extraneous or be given less attention.

Here it is enough to counsel caution on the side-effects of testing and to suggest that evaluation which takes a broader view of pupil achievement and pays more attention to process may lead, in the long term, to a form of accountability that reflects the quality and breadth of learning and teaching.

Process evaluation in practice in schools

In the last section of this paper I want to focus on some of the practical difficulties teachers encounter conducting evaluations in their own schools. Indirectly, these provide support for the three main arguments of this paper:

1 that evaluation should be a continuing part of professional practice;
2 that it needs to be separated for a time from accountability demands;
3 that in the long term it may lead toward a form of accountability consistent with professionalism.

The difficulties were first highlighted by a group of teachers who conducted a process study of one aspect of school policy as part of a course in school-based evaluation. They have since been tested out and/or observed through other courses jointly convened or attended by myself and involving in total some two hundred teachers from both primary and secondary schools.

The initial context in which the observations arose may be important for understanding the problems encountered. A brief description follows.

For two terms (a total of twenty weeks) twelve teachers, a mixture of primary and secondary and all senior in the school (heads, deputy heads or heads of department) attended a course run by myself which introduced them to the concepts and techniques of evaluation, the analysis and reporting of results.

A central feature of the course was the production of an evaluation study of a policy issue conducted by participants in their own schools. 'Policy issue' was interpreted widely to include issues relating to the curriculum, organization, management, teaching and learning at pupil, teacher, classroom, department or school level. Perhaps because of their role in the school or my bias in focusing on school evaluation rather more than on teacher or pupil evaluation, most participants chose an issue which had repercussions for a large number of staff in the school. Sixth form provision and privileges, mathematics policy review, and parental involvement in homework were three of the areas chosen for evaluation. Most chose to use the evaluation study as a starting point for discussion of the issue within the school. In giving teachers permission to attend the course the head had to agree to the study being undertaken. The aim of setting up the course in this way was to involve the teachers in the process of conducting an evaluation and producing a report while they were attending the course. Data from their evaluations were used for study during the course itself.

To the second session they were asked to bring a two hundred word statement of an evaluation problem in their school. They were encouraged to start their studies early, i.e. by the fourth week either with this problem or another, and invited to complete them two weeks before the course ended to be shared for discussion of data-analysis and skills of reporting.

At the first session we discussed people's expectations and motives for undertaking the course. These varied from self-development, curiosity, an awareness that evaluation was the 'in-topic', 'technique-gathering', to 'I was asked to come by the head'. At the end of the course we discussed their experience and their perceptions of progress. Throughout I documented their reactions to the process of doing an evaluation, the issues they found problematic and the questions they raised. Early in the third term, I interviewed several of the course members at length about their experience and subsequent action, if any, since the course.

There are three features of the course which differ from the notion of school self-evaluation outlined in this paper. One is that only one person from each school attended the course. Though, in some cases, they involved other members of the school in the evaluation, the responsibility for conducting and completing the evaluation lay with one person, not a group within the school. Secondly, while the evaluation studies took place within school, the course was off-site. Thirdly, the school did not generate the study; the stimulus was the course.

Observations

1   Teachers involved in process evaluation of their own schools do not readily respond to the notion of building upon 'natural practice' (Walker, 1974). Given a formal responsibility for evaluation they seek a corresponding formality in the means of data collection and analysis. Rather than a disciplined extension of their existing repertoire of skills and practices, such as intelligent questioning, observation and informed judgements, they look initially to the models of survey and experimental research for instrumentation. The effect is to deskill the teacher-evaluator in a manner akin to that observed by Mac-Donald (1973) in teachers experimenting with a novel pedagogy. In these circumstances theoretical explications of the parallels between systematic process evaluation and teacher decision-making may convince intellectually, but some period of immersion in the evaluation role is required

before the resemblance begins to be seen in their developing evaluation practice.

Partly this is a matter of confidence, partly a matter of prudence. Instruments such as questionnaires not only have the appeal of research respectability, they offer depersonalization of enquiry and distance from the potentially disruptive and alienating effects of close-up observation and questioning. In the early stages of an internal evaluation, political survival may be problematic and may seem to depend upon the adoption of relatively unthreatening approaches. Over time the deficiencies of such instruments, particularly for those who want to get at the social construction of curriculum realities, lead to their abandonment in favour of more qualitative approaches once the evaluation activity has gained an institutional niche.

2   Despite exhibiting a generalized nervousness about initiating an evaluation process in their schools, teachers fail to anticipate the need for carefully thought out and negotiated procedures governing access to and release of data. Typically it is not until the teacher-evaluator encounters difficulties in collecting data or objections to the evaluation from other members of staff that the political complexity of the activity crystallizes and compels him to think through the conditions of his institutional 'contract' and that set up for the evaluation.

3   The experience of school self-evaluation confirms Elliott and Adelman's findings from action research that teachers lack a precise enough language through which they can share their professional concerns (Elliott and Adelman (1976), Adelman and Elliott (1975)). Language refinement, especially to gain equivalence of meaning, is a daunting task for the teacher-evaluator who has successfully generated in his colleagues an awareness of shared problems and an interest in exploring them. This may also help to explain why teachers are reluctant to analyse and identify the criteria underlying their intuitive professional judgements in the classroom, or to give accounts of their

teaching that might illuminate the processes of pedagogy and schooling. It is certainly not the relevance of such accounts that is at issue, for teachers are well aware of the need, in the face of contemporary pressure for performance-based assessment, to generate evidence of the quality of the learning opportunities they seek to design. School self-evaluation gives them a chance to think through and operationalize the criteria by which they would want to be evaluated, but it will take time to develop the discourse and the forms of evidence that would adequately realize their convictions.

4 Constraints on school self-evaluation frequently cited by teachers are time and motivation. Most teachers do not feel they have enough time to engage in this 'additional' activity, and few are prepared to give it a high priority, especially where, as is often the case, there is no firm commitment on the part of the school hierarchy to consider the results. Although many regard official formulae for assessing school performance with some hostility, the threat of external auditing is insufficient to motivate teachers into active exploration of alternative practices.

It seems that some catalyst from within or from outside the school is needed to provide the initial stimulus and continuing support for self-evaluation. Within the school it may be that the deputy head is the most likely candidate for such a role. He has a whole-school responsibility, so that his interest is seen to be legitimate; teachers, on the other hand, often see their major responsibility to be their classroom or, in secondary schools, their subject. Interest in whole-school evaluation is often not perceived by them, their colleagues or senior management as a central facet of their role. Whether it should be is a separate issue for the school to discuss. Teachers may be classroom or subject teachers first, but are they not also members of the whole school? Do not decisions made at school level effect decisions at classroom level and the quality of teaching? The case for school self-evaluation (see pages 119–20) rests on assumptions like these of the school as a community with overlapping and interrelated interests.

Legitimacy of concern is an important factor in the acceptability of an in-school evaluator and a serious constraint on individual teachers who want to extend their evaluation interests beyond the boundary of their own professional responsibilities. The deputy has dual access, to the teachers and the head, and if he enjoys the confidence of both is well placed to initiate the evaluation process.

Objections may be raised to the managerial aspect of his role and doubts are sometimes expressed about the use that may be made of the evaluation by the management structure. But where the purpose of the evaluation and the procedures for gathering and exchange of information are clear and the confidence expressed above exists, such doubts may be short-lived. The deputy head may also be an ally in the creation of time, space and whole-school strategies for the discussion and utilization of the evaluation. Legitimacy has another aspect related to specific interests and respect of persons. Teachers indicated that sometimes the most appropriate person to be an in-school evaluator was one who had responsibility for influencing policy in that specific area (i.e. the person in charge of the sixth form might be the best person to study sixth form provision; the head of the pastoral system the best person to study the pastoral system). Against this, however, others claimed that a disinterested person or team would be more appropriate. In practice decisions as to who is the most legitimate person/s to initiate and/or conduct a school self-evaluation will be determined on the basis of local knowledge of the context and relationships. What is important is that the person or team selected is seen by the whole school to be credible and competent to undertake the evaluation.

Outside the school, in-service education, the context in

which these observations first arose, provides a catalyst for
initial development and continuing support.

5   Experience suggests that teachers engaged in school
self-evaluation require support to sustain the exercise.
Specifically, support seems essential in the following
ways:

(a)   *in-service course support* on the need for evaluation, the concepts of evaluation, and the advantages and
disadvantages of different approaches;

(b)   *on-site support* in the form of acceptance by the
head and colleagues of the relevance and importance of
the exercise and the need to create time to pursue aspects
of the evaluation and/or a structure to discuss the issues for
evaluation progress reports and results;

(c)   *intermittent or continuing consultancy support* in
the form of outside advice on specific aspects of the evaluation – design, testing, interviewing, processing data, or
whatever is most needed by the school at different times;

(d)   *off-site support* in the form of regular meetings
with teachers/teams from other schools to share experience and back-up services – reprographic, typing, duplica-
tion of case studies, etc., to facilitate this process;

(e)   *LEA support* in terms of in-service courses mentioned above, extra resources to buy in release time, consultancy or material support and realistic expectations of
the time needed to build up skills and confidence in the
process.

6   Credibility is an issue in all forms of public reporting
but is particularly acute, or felt to be acute, in self-
reporting. Concern is expressed as much by insiders
(whether taking part in the evaluation or not) as outsiders
(readers of reports outside the immediate school environment). Objections revolve around the subjective nature of
the observations, the political context or self-interest of
the reporters and their expertise. Credibility is problematic in the current political context where certain kinds of

information are valued and sought by people outside the school.

In time, credibility may cease to be an issue as more self-reports become available and are seen to be useful. For the moment, however, when the criteria for assessing the worth of such reports have yet to evolve, some form of external validation may be necessary to secure credibility.

There are at least three different roles an external person or group could assume. One is the role of a critical friend, a second is a consultant on the design and methods of evaluation, and a third is a judge or arbiter of the outcomes of an evaluation.

The notion of external audit has also been suggested as one way of monitoring or offering credibility to self-accounts. This notion is not dissimilar from the accreditation procedures employed in America. The school first evaluates itself on criteria that are drawn up by the accreditation agency; the agency then visits and carries out an evaluation and, on the basis of the evaluations, decides whether the school should be accredited. Though I have not looked at this system in detail, a critical question which arises in relation to school self-evaluation is the extent to which schools are free to produce accounts on criteria other than those determined by the agency, or the extent to which the priorities and self-perceptions of the school are represented in the criteria drawn up by the agency.

Much depends upon how the concept is interpreted in practice. If an audit focuses upon an examination of the rigour with which the evaluation has been conducted, checking for biases and establishing the adequacy of descriptions according to criteria which are shared, this is likely to be perceived differently from an audit which attempts to be the final judge of the worth of the contents. The first interpretation is most conducive, I would argue, to the professional development of the school; the second, more likely to create anxiety and defensiveness and run the risk of becoming yet another external evaluation, albeit one which gives the school some choice of criteria and the first say.

Assuming for the moment that some form of external consultancy or critique is desirable, who would offer such consultancy or critique? There are a variety of people one could employ (advisers, higher education lecturers, teachers, for example) from a range of institutions; and different people might be sought at different stages of the evaluation for different purposes. The logical conclusion to the argument raised in this paper is that the school should decide who any such person might be.

The role of the adviser is perhaps the most problematic. Advisers form an important part of the structure of the service and an external support role could be seen to be an integral part of their job. Yet they also frequently have a role to play in assessing promotion prospects. The multiplicity of roles may conflict. It may be possible for advisers to detach themselves from their promotional role in order to support or criticize an evaluation, but it may not be easy or perceived to be the case by those involved in the evaluation. The problem of detachment is true for other people who may take an external role, too, but the potential adverse effects are not the same or perceived to be the same when these people are not in a position directly or indirectly to affect the careers of the people involved.

It is often assumed that outsiders will be more objective and that this in itself lends credibility to self-reports. Whether or not this is so depends upon the knowledge individuals have of the subject and context, the degree to which they are personally objective, the insight they have into the processes of learning and schooling and the evaluation skills they possess. Outsiders may perceive things differently and this in itself may be helpful, but it cannot be equated with objectivity. In the end local knowledge may determine who is the best person to undertake a supportive role or constructive critique.

In short, the person is more important than the role, although some roles have more dangers inherent in them than others. What is crucial is that those who are assessing the credibility of the evaluation (whether it be parents, local community, governors or LEA) respect the validator whoever he/she may be.

If self-evaluation were to be instituted as part of a local or national structure it would be tidy to nominate or designate a group of persons to fulfil this external role. The difficulties with advisers have already been mentioned. Peer evaluation would seem to present less of a problem. It is most consistent with the professional argument and is also perceived to be less threatening by teachers. Certainly, given a choice of what group of people could best provide an external critique, many teachers have suggested that peer evaluation is the most desirable.

Conclusion

The initial difficulties experienced by teachers in conducting self-evaluations for public scrutiny, whether that public be professional colleagues or the outside community, plus the need to build up confidence in the process both within and outside the school, constitute a strong case for separating the development of school self-evaluation on process criteria from accountability demands on a traditional model. One form of evaluation cannot serve the purposes for which the other form is invoked. It is inappropriate, in fact, to compare the two since they operate on completely different assumptions. And it would be inappropriate to use a form of process evaluation as an accountability mechanism before the criteria for the production and acceptance of such evaluations were widely shared. Had school self-evaluation been initiated ten years ago, or even five, schools might be in a position to use it as a form of accountability now. As it is, it has taken the threat of external accountability to raise interest in systematic school self-evaluation (a fact that has not gone unnoticed by many teachers now concerned about the testing initiatives of central government (*TES*, 15 Feb. 1980)) and to encourage teachers to assert the autonomy granted to them in rhetoric and, to a considerable degree, in reality.

External support, in the form of in-service course and release time on and off site, now seems necessary if schools are to evaluate their practice to a point where it can become a viable form of accountability. The process will take time. But it will only begin to take place at all if the system becomes more, not less, open and demonstrates a commitment towards the sharing of information between different sectors of the service.

References

Adelman, C. & Elliott, J. (1975) Practitioners' language of teaching. *New Era* **56** (5) June, 106–10.

Cronbach, L. (1975) Beyond the two disciplines of scientific psychology. *American Psychologist* **30** February, 116–27.

Elliott, J. (1978a) Who should monitor performance in schools? (Paper first presented at Association for the Study of the Curriculum Conference, March 1978). In H. Sockett (1980) *Accountability in the English Educational System*. London: Hodder & Stoughton.

—— (1978b) Classroom accountability and the self-monitoring teacher. In W. Harlen (ed.) (1978) *Evaluation and the Teacher's Role*. London: Macmillan.

—— (1979) The self-assessment of teacher performance. In *Classroom Action Research Network*, Bulletin **3**, Spring 1979. Cambridge Institute of Education.

—— & Adelman, C. (1976) Innovation at the Classroom Level: a case study of the Ford Teaching Project. In

Curriculum Design and Development E203, Unit **28**, 52–64. Milton Keynes: Open University Press.

Goldstein, H. (1979) The Mystification of Assessment. *Forum* **22** (1), 14–16.

Goldstein, H. & Blinkhorn, S. (1977) Monitoring educational standards: an inappropriate model. *Bulletin of the British Psychological Society* **30**, 309–11.

—— (1979a) Pupil assessment. In *Classroom Action Research Network*, Bulletin 3, Spring 1979. Cambridge Institute of Education.

—— (1979b) Accountability that is of benefit to schools. *Journal of Curriculum Studies* **2** (4), 287–97.

Harlen, W. (ed.) (1978) *Evaluation and the Teacher's Role*, ch. 1. London: Macmillan.

House, E. R. (1973a) The price of productivity: who pays? University of Illinois, mimeo.

—— (ed.) (1973b) *School Evaluation: The Politics and the Process*. Berkeley, Calif: McCutchan.

—— (1979) The objectivity, fairness, and justice of federal evaluation policy as reflected in the Follow Through Evaluation. *Educational Evaluation and Policy Analysis* **1** (1), 28–42.

MacDonald, B. (1973) Innovation and incompetence. In D. Hamingson (ed.) *Towards Judgement; The Publications of the Evaluation Unit of the Humanities Curriculum Project 1970–72. CARE, University of East Anglia, Occasional Paper No.* **1**, 89–92.

—— (1978) Accountability, standards and the process of schooling. In T. Becher & S. Maclure *Accountability in Education*. Slough: NFER.

Parlett, M. & Hamilton, D. (1972) Evaluation as illumination: a new approach to the study of innovatory programmes. In D. Hamilton *et al*. (eds.) (1977) *Beyond the Numbers Game*. London: Macmillan Education.

Read, L. F. (1973) An assessment of the Michigan assessment. In E. R. House (ed.) (1973b) *School Evaluation: The Politics and the Process*, 60–73. Berkeley,

Calif.: McCutchan.

Simons, H. (1978) School-based evaluation on democratic principles. In *Classroom Action Research Network*, Bulletin 2, January. Cambridge Institute of Education.

—— (1980) The evaluative school. *Forum* 22 (2), 55–7.

Stake, R. E. (1967) The Countenance of Educational Evaluation. In *Teachers College Record* 68 (7), 523–40.

—— (1976) Making school evaluations relevant. *North Central Association Quarterly* 50 (4), 347–52.

—— (1978) More subjective! Paper submitted as part of an invited debate at AERA, Division D, March 1978, 'Should Educational Evaluation Be More Objective or More Subjective?' University of Illinois, mimeo.

Stenhouse, L. (1975) *An Introduction to Curriculum Research and Development*, ch. 10. London: Heinemann Educational.

Walker, R. (1974) Classroom research: a view from SAFARI. In *SAFARI, Innovation, Evaluation, Research and the Problem of Control: Some Interim Papers*. CARE, University of East Anglia.

Part Two

6   Introduction to Part Two

Denis Lawton

A good deal of the discussion about accountability in this section centres on one peculiarly British institution – the Assessment of Performance Unit (APU). It may be useful to begin by describing the origin and development of this unit, and then proceed to a discussion of the issues which have emerged, and are still emerging, as a result of this kind of exercise in monitoring. One of the more general issues which arises from the specific context of the APU is the problem of comparability: how can standards be compared over periods of time? The problem exists even in the supposedly 'content free' area of intelligence testing. If a test were devised, standardized and first used on a group of eleven-year-olds in 1950, and exactly the same test were used on a corresponding group in 1970, the average scores would not necessarily be the same. The average score in 1950 would have to be 100; if the average in 1970 dropped to 95 it would be wrong to assume that intelligence was necessarily declining. A more likely explanation would be that some test items devised in 1950 were out of date by 1970 and, therefore, more difficult. For this reason intelligence tests are regularly brought up to date – but there is, of course, no guarantee that the new items are of *exactly* the same level of difficulty as the original items. The only method for updating tests ensures that they cannot be used reliably over long periods of time. The method used is to restandardize against a contemporary population. The assumption built into this process is that the contemporary population is of the same intelligence as the old. It is difficult therefore to know whether or not intelligence is declining. The same kind of problem exists in comparing standards of reading, arithmetic and other subjects over a period of time. Item banking and the Rasch model are attempts that have been made to overcome this problem. They will be described in detail below, together with some of the methodological problems which still exist. Item banking and the Rasch model have been proposed as possible answers to the APU's difficult task of comparing educational standards.

The origin and development of the APU

The intention to form a unit concerned with the assessment of performance of school pupils was mentioned by Reginald Prentice, at that time a Labour Party Secretary of State for Education, in a speech to the National Association of School Masters' Conference in April 1974. An official announcement soon followed (in August 1974) in the White Paper *Educational Disadvantage and the Educational Needs of Immigrants* (Command 5720). The White Paper was the response by the Department of Education and Science to the Report on Education by a House of Commons Select Committee on race relations and immigration.

There is some evidence to suggest, however, that the APU or something like it was being planned several years before 1974, but the DES may have realized that a proposal to monitor standards nationally would have faced strong resistance from the teaching profession. However, to assess the special needs of disadvantaged children is much less offensive to the profession. Thus the proposal for a national testing programme appeared as part of a programme for the educationally disadvantaged and the APU this time was closely connected with the Educational Disadvantage Unit (EDU).

The terms of reference of the APU are:

To promote the development of methods of assessing and monitoring the achievement of children at school, and to seek to identify the incidence of under-achievement.

This brief, and somewhat ambiguous, statement is amplified in the following way:

The tasks laid down are:

1   To identify and appraise existing instruments and methods of assessment which may be relevant for these purposes.

2   To sponsor the creation of new instruments and techniques for assessment, having due regard to statistical and sampling methods.

3   To promote the conduct of assessment in co-operation with local education authorities and teachers.

4   To identify significant differences of achievement related to the circumstances in which children learn, including the incidence of under-achievement, and to make the findings available to those concerned with resource allocation within the Department, local education authorities and schools.

Even the clarification of the terms of reference by these four tasks are still sufficiently vague to enable the APU to develop in a way very different from the original association with immigrant and disadvantaged children. As the years passed more emphasis was placed on assessment of standards and monitoring, and less on the needs of disadvantaged children. In the Green Paper (July 1977) the reference made to APU comes under the heading 'standards and assessment'. By this time also there is a clear indication that local education authorities will undertake separate kinds of monitoring:

> 3.10. The departments are concerned with assessing individual pupils only as members of a representative sample, and this is the major function of the APU. A number of educational authorities have already decided on or are considering monitoring the performance of pupils in their areas: tests suitable for this purpose are likely to come out of the work of the APU. Here again the departments' concern is that there should be consistency within local education authorities and wherever possible between authorities.

During 1977 and 1978 five explanatory leaflets and two subject booklets (on mathematics and language) were produced by the DES/APU. None of them mention educational disadvantage. One of them (*APU: An Introduction*) gives this explanation:

> The last ten years have seen changes in school organization and curriculum. We need to be able to monitor the consequences of children's performance in school. We need to know how our schools are serving the changing needs of children and society. That is why the Department of Education and Science set up the APU.

It is interesting to note that the APU featured in the very brief section on education in the 1979 Conservative Party Election Manifesto:

> We shall promote higher standards of achievement in basic skills. The Government's Assessment of Performance Unit will set national standards in reading, writing and arithmetic, monitored by tests worked out with teachers and others and applied locally by education authorities.

Since the Conservative Party won the 1979 General Election, it must be supposed that the above quotation now represents official government policy. This establishes a connection between questions of accountability raised in the first part of this book and the functioning of the APU. The policy of 'setting' national standards must presumably refer to minimum levels of competency in the basic skills, and this in turn relates to discussions about mastery learning.

Issues – philosophical, statistical and political

Any attempt to measure educational performance across the whole curriculum has to use some kind of model. In England the problem is made more difficult by the fact that there is no national, compulsory curriculum, and schools are, in theory, free to use any curriculum they choose. The APU attempted to solve this difficulty by proposing to test children's *development* in six areas (language, mathematics, science, aesthetic, social and personal, physical). Schools could teach whatever they wanted; the APU had no desire to influence the curriculum – only to monitor pupils' development in those six areas. Richard Pring points out some of the very important philosophical difficulties in the stance adopted by the APU in this respect. More recently, it has been suggested that two additional areas of development should be considered: modern languages and technology; this suggestion illustrates some of the difficulty associated with 'six areas', but if two additions are introduced they will pose considerable further difficulties.

This takes us on to the very difficult area of item banking. An 'item' is usually defined as a question for which the correct answer can be pre-specified so that any competent marker will grade an answer, correct or incorrect, without difficulty. A 'bank' is a collection of test items which can be used in different combinations to construct parallel tests, the scores of which can be compared. The Rasch model, named after the Danish mathematician, Georg Rasch (1960), is one of several statistical models used to describe performance on tests composed of a number of different items. These items are assumed to have one right answer and one or more wrong answers, so that a subject attempting the test either 'passes' or 'fails' each item. The characteristic feature of the model is that it assumes that only two quantities are needed to determine the probability of a subject passing an item; his 'ability', assumed to be the same regardless of which item in the test is being attempted, and the 'difficulty' of the item, assumed to be the same regardless of who is attempting it. Given these two quantities, the ratio of the probability of a correct response to the probability of an incorrect response is assumed to be directly proportional to the individual's ability multiplied by the item's difficulty. If the assumptions hold, it follows that, for all subjects, a set of items will all be ranked in the same order of difficulty irrespective of other individual characteristics. Initially, of course, individual ability and item difficulty are not given: they have to be estimated. Similarly, it might not be expected that all test items would fall into a single scale, rather a number of scales would be needed, certainly across broad subject areas (mathematics, English, etc.) and probably within such areas. The construction of a set of such scales based on large numbers of items (an 'item bank') involves both the sorting of items into scales, and the estimation, by appropriate computational techniques, of the difficulties of the items and the abilities of the individuals, using an initial base-line sample. The accuracy of the estimation of item difficulties depends on the number of individuals answering each item, and the accuracy of the estimation of the ability of each individual likewise depends on the number of items which contribute to his score. The item difficulties obtained are then used as the basis for the future allocation of scores to individuals who take tests composed of items selected from the bank.

Harvey Goldstein begins by discussing two problems for testers: first, how to devise tests which are fair to pupils who have been taught by different curricula and methods; second, the problem of tests getting out of date. Goldstein then proceeds to look at the Rasch model which has sometimes been suggested for use by the APU. He finds the model sadly wanting. Part of the argument here is statistical, but part of it is more basic; Goldstein suggests that there are fundamental weaknesses in the thinking behind the Rasch model. In particular, he argues that an item bank based on Rasch is inherently unworkable.

Graham Tall joins in the attack on the Rasch model as a basis for item banks and school examinations. He is particularly concerned with the problem of backlash: the APU officers have claimed that their tests will not affect the curriculum in any way, but Tall argues that this is impossible in the real world of schools, teachers and pupils. He also shows that not only is the curriculum likely to be distorted by the tests, but that in the long run teaching methods may also be at risk. Tall attacks the Rasch model on grounds of pretentiousness: the model purports to be more precise than it is, and claims to measure something it cannot.

In the next section we give an opportunity to Bruce Choppin of the National Foundation for Educational Research to come to the defence of the item bank model. Choppin begins by making a sharp distinction between *measurement* and 'assessment, examination, evaluation or ranking'. Measurement implies quantification and objectivity – presumably not bad things to have in education. Choppin asks opponents not to over-simplify and misrepresent the position of those educationists, like him, who want to make the best use possible of admittedly imperfect measuring instruments. The basic problem seems to be that the kind of measurement advocated by Choppin is, of necessity, one-dimensional (measurement he claims must be!), whereas educational processes are essentially multi-dimensional. This is the real conflict between the item bankers and those who oppose Rasch and similar models. If you want to measure you must pay a certain price (precision implies austerity); if you prefer instead to assess or evaluate, then you sacrifice accuracy, reliability and objectivity. Choppin concludes by making an appeal that we should not abandon measurement altogether, and he lists three valuable roles for educational measurement (one of them being 'monitoring standards'). Models such as Rasch should not be seen as true or false, but as adequate or inadequate, and Choppin suggests that it would be a great folly to abandon measurement and item banks simply because they do not provide final answers to our educational problems.

At this point, we are back to the main issue which divided the contributors to the first section of this book. The problem is that any system of measurement is necessarily a simplification; as such, it is useful but dangerous. Everything depends on the way that the measurement is used. If the community invests too much importance in a single, simple measurement of educational achievement then there is a danger that education will be distorted, and that a useful diagnostic device is lost to teachers – the test becomes the main objective for pupils, their parents and teachers, rather than a means of diagnosing particular difficulties and aptitudes.

References

Atkin, J. M. (1979) Educational accountability in the United States. *Educational Analysis* 1 (1).
Becher, T. (1979) Self-accounting, evaluation and accountability. *Educational Analysis* 1 (1).

Bloom, (ed.) (1956) *The Taxonomy of Educational Objectives*. London: Longman.

Dahllof, U. (1979) The classroom complexities behind the test scores: some Swedish experiences. *Educational Analysis* **1** (1).

Elliott, J. (1979) Accountability, progressive education and school-based evaluation. *Education 3—13*.

Elliott, J. (1980) Who should monitor performance in schools? In Sockett (1980).

Eraut, M. (1977) Accountability at School Level. Mimeo, University of Sussex.

Gray, (1979) The statistics of accountability. *Education Policy Bulletin* **7** (1).

Lessinger, L. M. (1972) Accountability for results: a basic challenge for America's schools. In J. M. Lessinger and R. W. Tyler (eds.) *Accountability in Education*. Washington, Ohio: Charles A. Jones.

MacDonald, B. (1978) Accountability, standards and the process of schooling. Mimeo, University of East Anglia.

Sockett, H. (ed.) (1980) *Accountability in the English Educational System*. London: Hodder & Stoughton.

Tyler, R. (1949) *Basic Principles of Curriculum Instruction*. University of Chicago Press.

7 Monitoring performance: reflections on the Assessment of Performance Unit*

Richard Pring

The main purpose of the APU is to devise ways of assessing, in very broad terms, the effectiveness of the educational system, and to do this by monitoring pupils' performance *across the curriculum* at different ages.

Several points need to be made clear about the work of the APU. First, the unit is not concerned with standards, but with a broad picture of performance so that any public discussion of standards might be better informed. Second, the unit will not be able to identify the performance of individual pupils, schools or authorities, although it may provide the sort of base from which individual schools or authorities may look at their own performance. Third, it is not an evaluation of the curriculum, although it might provide the basis for deciding where 'in depth' evaluation studies are needed and where resources should be allocated.

Given these general aims, the first major step in the unit's thinking was to devise an adequate 'curriculum model'. Since it aimed to assess *across the curriculum*, the model would need to reflect the many different activities that teachers engage in. But how could one tidy these

*This paper was originally written in 1978, though altered in 1979, before it was decided not to monitor personal and social development.

many diverse curriculum activities, reflected in a multitude of different aims and subject-matters, into a coherent yet simple model of curriculum?

The model adopted was that of six areas or lines of development which transcend particular subject boundaries: mathematical, language, scientific, physical, aesthetic, and personal and social. A seventh area was subsequently added, namely that of modern languages, and a working group was set up to investigate the extent to which 'design and technology' was an area in need of assessment, quite distinct from the others mentioned. The argument was that, whatever the range of subject-matters taught, and whatever the differences in content, everything contributes to one or more of these areas of development. Thus the subject 'history' would contribute to language development, possibly to scientific, to personal and social development, and so on. On the other hand, no specific curriculum experience is a *necessary* condition for any one line of development. Hence, we have a model for monitoring pupil performance across the curriculum and across the country, which (it is claimed) does not determine what should be taught in schools. It is claimed to be a national system of assessment compatible with the much cherished autonomy of the schools.

The procedure adopted by the APU was to establish working groups for each of the 'lines of development'. These groups would identify the main strands of development which would reflect the curriculum aims and activities of schools – whatever the balance of subjects or the differences in curriculum content between one school and another. Then the unit would fund research within each area to discover ways of monitoring performance on a 'light sampling' basis. At the time of writing, a report has been published on the first attempt to monitor in the area of mathematics. Monitoring has taken place in language but not yet reported upon. This year it is intended to monitor in science. Decisions have yet to be made about monitoring in the other areas, and especially in the area of personal and social development there is some pressure from the teachers' representatives *not* to proceed.

Finally, by way of introduction, it should be noted that a major aim of the APU is to provide the basis for comparison over time. Without such a basis, the often stated view that standards are declining will remain mere opinion. The difficulties however of longitudinal comparison are considerable – they are set out clearly in chapters 3 and 4 of the Bullock Report (1975). It is in the attempt to meet these difficulties that interest has been shown in the Rasch model, a mathematical procedure that (so it is claimed) meets the problem in longitudinal comparisons stemming from changing cultural patterns and interests. Several of the contributions to this book examine the problems that lie in adopting this model, and thus in fulfilling the aim of the APU to make valid comparisons over time. The significance of the controversy, however, needs to be kept in perspective. Comparison over time is but one aim of the APU. Furthermore, the adoption of the Rasch model is by no means indispensable. Comparison of performance can be achieved by a detailed and continually updated account of what is happening in schools, even though the comparison between two accounts would lack the grounds for precision that a mathematical model is thought by some to give. The major aim of the APU, however it is expressed in detail, is not to provide 'the objective' account of what happens or a definitive statement of whether standards are rising or declining. Rather does it aim to give a more detailed picture of what is achieved so that judgements made about schools can be more objective than they otherwise would be. Politicians, administrators, teachers and parents do make judgements about schools, and some of these judgements are comparative ones over time. The APU cannot provide definitive answers to questions raised, and indeed should not aim to do so. It can, however, provide a more informed basis upon which to make those judgements – or indeed upon which to challenge those judgements once they are made. In that sense the work of the APU should be seen as *part*, and no more, of the evidence upon which a more objective account of schooling can be given.

Although I remain in broad agreement with the aims of the APU, I do see certain, as yet unresolved, problems in its approach to monitoring which, though less technical than those raised in subsequent contributions to this book, are possibly more fundamental. These concern:

1   the adoption of a particular curriculum model;
2   the focus upon development;
3   the distinction between form and content;
4   the selection of objectives.

The adoption of a particular curriculum model

The unit has identified six lines or areas of development but each of these is likely to include a wide range of developments that, in many cases, are only loosely inter-connected, if connected at all. For instance, 'social and personal' would include the development of responsibility in carrying out commitments, of the *feeling* of responsibility for others in need of help, of moral reasoning and judgement, of many different virtues (each of which might constitute an independent line of development), of social sensitivity, of religious awareness, and so on – indefinitely. There is clearly an enormous amount of conceptual map-work to be done, as well as links to be made between emotions, motives and cognitions, before one can justifiably talk about *a* particular area of development. Failure to do this conceptual work would cast doubt upon the identification of six rather than eight, nine or twenty areas of development. For without further argument the choice of six 'areas' does seem rather arbitrary, just as the identification of six 'realms of meaning' or seven 'forms of knowledge' remains unconvincing without adequate philosophical justification. The point is that distinctions *within* areas might be as important for assessment purposes as distinctions *between* areas, but that, in organizing one's distinctions in this hierarchical way rather than in another, one may get a distorted analysis of the many sorts of activities one is trying to assess.

A great deal of philosophical literature has recently been devoted to organizing curriculum knowledge into fundamentally different kinds. Phenix (1964) proposes six realms of meaning, Hirst (1965) argues for seven forms of knowledge. I however have remained unconvinced of the philosophical force of their arguments. Firstly, the development of human knowledge and understanding is manifested in a variety of forms, even at the common-sense level, many of which have been developed in a disciplined and systematic way. The resulting disciplines do not fit neatly into a few major forms or categories, though each will resemble and interconnect with others in a variety of ways. Somehow the richness of the various modes of thinking and operating can get lost in the reduction of all this to a few major categories, just as history for Phenix becomes historicism (the study of the totality of facts), and the fine arts for Hirst become kinds of proposition though of a peculiar sort.

This may not matter too much. Some model needs to be adopted if the variety of curriculum activities is not to be submerged under the pressure for testing in 'basics' only. It would not matter if these are seen as rough classifications only (although the fewer the classifications the rougher they must be) and if the distinctions between what is contained within each classification are not neglected in the pursuit of simplicity and coherence. But the classification is not acknowledged by the APU to be pragmatic in this sense, and certain parts of the curriculum, in order to be made to fit, are thereby in danger of changing character or of being neglected. Let us take some examples. Social science is taught through several subjects – economics, anthropology, social studies, sociology. It has, of course, features in common with the natural sciences, but to subsume it within the natural sciences would be to beg a key question about the distinctive nature of explaining social events. It is questionable whether the sorts of development that natural and social scientists are respectively trying to foster might be characterized in such similar ways. Or again design and technology do seem to make distinctive demands upon human practical ingenuity, and yet its elevation to an area for assessment has been resisted on the grounds that its various parts fall within the scope of other groups. Perhaps upon analysis they do, and that might be the final conclusion of the APU, but the practical knowledge or 'know-how' exercised in design and technology is more than the aggregate of these different parts, and thus if treated in that way they would in essence be neglected. Or, again, historians would claim something distinctive about their own discipline, however disunited they may be in giving an account of it. And the neglect of this distinctiveness in the likening of history to the social and natural sciences, or in putting it into the area of personal and social development, might create a model of assessment that does not capture some of the important things that have been excellently taught. My difficulty is that I am not as convinced as many seem to be that curriculum subjects are so arbitrary in the divisions of knowledge they embody that they can be allowed to get lost in a comprehensive monitoring of curriculum performance.

Focus upon lines of development

The APU from the start has expressed its interest in lines or areas of *development*, in contrast to subjects. The reason for this was indicated in my opening paragraphs. The problem for the APU, as for anyone adopting a similar curriculum model, is that of defending a description of curriculum achievement, whether or not for purposes of assessment, that transcends particular curriculum content (and thus the wide variations that arise from a diversified curriculum). To talk of lines of development is part of the search for some general characterization of the development of the mind, of its powers and qualities, that would be compatible with a wider range of different judgements about worthwhile content.

The APU however has never stated clearly what it means by development and this is of some practical importance. Let me illustrate the different meanings and the practical significance of adopting any one of them.

In its strong sense 'development' implies that some change has taken place in which later stages of thinking 'grow out' of earlier ones. The later stages both presuppose, and improve upon, the earlier ones. For example, the capacity for abstract and hypothetical thinking presupposes what Piaget refers to as the stage of concrete operations. Kohlberg and colleagues point to six stages of development in moral reasoning; moving from one stage to another is a *development* because, first, the general movement is towards a more valuable state of mind and, secondly, the later, more valuable, stages are somehow potentially already there in the earlier ones. They grow out of them; they are not learnt or acquired 'from outside'. Formal operations are already anticipated in the intuitive and concrete thinking of the young child; the universalized principles of justice are already anticipated in the four-year-old's quaint use of the word 'fair'. 'Development' is therefore contrasted with learning. Of course, particular learning experiences are required through which the quality of one's thinking will develop. But the development consists in the improvement of the potential quality of one's thinking rather than in having any particular thoughts. Following Kohlberg in the moral area, several people have explored the stage developments in the social awareness and perspectives of the child (Selman (1976), Damon (1977)).

Shorn of some of the more dubious philosophical claims (see Peters, 1971), this conception of development would seem to have much to commend it to the APU, especially in the area of personal and social development. But there are two major difficulties. Firstly, to adopt such a notion of development is to take on board a great deal of highly contentious theory. Secondly, its virtue is also its fault. In making a contrast between development and learning the mode of assessment would not unduly influence what is taught in schools; on the other hand (and for that very reason) it would say very little about what they had achieved.

There is a weaker sense of development that would distinguish between the process and the outcomes, and would argue that what counts as development depends upon the value one attaches to certain possible outcomes. Any process is a developmental one if early stages of the process can be shown empirically to lead to a set of outcomes that are held to be worthwhile. The report of the language working group has such a sense of development (APU, 1979). In stressing the functional aspect of reading and writing, it argues for a variety of tests that will reflect the several different functions of language and the adequacy of language performance for different kinds of audience. But this differentiation in performance, respecting both differences in function and differences in audience, is a matter of growth. 'As children grow older, their ability to match their writing to particular tasks and to particular contexts increases. Thus the tasks set to 15 year olds should be more differentiated than those set to 11 year olds'. Assumed is 'a general ability to communicate' which 'develops progressively more specific application for various tasks and various contexts'. There is a shift to more reflective, analytic writing. The language group regarded even this rather limited sense of development with caution. To a great extent it was an empirical matter. 'The framework . . . is no more than a set of hypotheses about those variations in

task and context that are likely to affect performance . . .
No doubt . . . some of the hypotheses will be shown to be
unfounded'.

It would be difficult to disagree with the particular values agreed by the language group that enter into its definition of development, namely, the gradual differentiation
both of language functions and of the sense of audience.
But such agreement in values is not so easily reached in
other areas, and this disagreement will be reflected in
differences of opinion about what a 'line of development'
consists of. Those supporting the weaker sense of development will need to agree what is of value, and what therefore constitutes the goal or end-state in terms of which
development is to be defined. To monitor the process of
development requires some prior decision about educational ends – what language attainments are worthwhile,
what is a socially developed person, what is to count as
numerate. And these decisions cannot be made either from
inspecting the process of development itself, as in the
strong sense of development, or from reflecting what is
going on in schools. But this is incompatible with the
adoption of a neutral stance – the monitoring simply of
what is. The APU therefore is necessarily in the business of
making value judgements about where schools should be
going.

A third sense of development seems at first sight to avoid
this, namely that assumed by a particular use of norm-
referenced tests. Certain tests might discriminate between
pupils of a certain age group, and, if properly standardized,
might give a set of norms for that group. If normal
achievement for that age group is compared with normal
achievement on similar items for a different age group, we
may get what would be regarded by some as a statistically
significant measurement of development. It is of course
the declared policy of the APU to engage in criterion rather
than norm-referenced testing. But a criterion-referenced
test can be norm-referenced should the assessors so wish.

And where lines of *development* are being monitored then, in the absence of other conceptions of development, the creation of norm-referenced tests for measuring longitudinal improvement would appear to be one way forward. It was not, for instance, the original intention of the National Assessment of Educational Progress in the USA to provide norm-referenced testing. However, by norm-referencing their tests in a particular way this is exactly what has happened, introducing as it did a particular notion of development. Although objectives were formulated by NAEP to make them specific to the four ages being assessed – nine years, thirteen years, seventeen years, and adult – two points should be noted: (a) items were sometimes chosen because, as a result of field testing, the assessors knew what proportion of each group were expected to 'succeed' – hence items were chosen for nine-year-olds that, say, 10 per cent, 50 per cent, and 90 per cent respectively would be able to answer, and (b) the same items would sometimes be chosen so that comparisons between ages could be made. In making the shift from 10 per cent to 50 per cent and then to 90 per cent mastery at different ages, developmental norms were established.

It is not clear then what sense of development the APU is using. However it is difficult to know what development could mean without it incorporating judgements of educational *improvement* from one age to another. And that involves much more than monitoring what is the case. It requires judgements of overall education aims and it requires judgements of how what happens at one age relates to subsequent performance at a later age.

The distinction between form and content

A major reason for a cross-curricular model was that the APU had to create a system of assessment reflecting what happened in school, despite the many differences in content and approach. It was assumed that there are relatively

few themes and upon these there might be infinite variations. A 'line of development', if identified, would enable
this to be done. Whatever the differences between one
curriculum and another in any one area to be assessed, the
respective curriculum contents would contribute to a
mode of thinking and/or behaving which 'lay beneath'
these differences. The notion of development, harking
back to *general qualities* of thinking that can be manifest
in a range of subjects and subject-matters, seems apt for
this particular approach.

Despite the importance of this distinction for the work of
the APU – namely, between specific curriculum content
on the one hand and the general qualities or processes of
thinking on the other – it has never as far as I know been
fully explored. The difficulties come across fairly clearly in
the thinking of the science group (APU, 1977):

> Science is therefore regarded as a term which describes
> particular ways of thinking about and tackling problems
> rather than as a label to cover particular school subjects.
> It follows that the monitoring of science lays emphasis
> on the particular processes and skills which should be
> the distinctive outcomes of science education . . . it
> should not be confined to biology, chemistry and phys-
> ics. (p. 2)

These processes ('Science activity categories'), common to
the different levels and contents of science, are listed later
in the group's thinking (APU, 1979) as:

Using symbolic representation
Using apparatus and measuring instruments
Observation
Interpretations and Application
Design of investigation
Performing investigation

These different processes, however, do appear in this later
publication of the steering group alongside a list of 'con-

cept areas' and contexts. Once one gets beyond a very elementary level in science it is difficult to see what a *scientific* observation or interpretation or enquiry would look like unless it did incorporate a particular conceptual framework and thus a particular theoretical position. The abstraction of processes from scientific activity is conceptually possible for certain purposes (e.g. systematizing the check list for evaluating science learning) but as such it is but an abstraction and does not describe 'doing science'. Therefore there has been within the science exploratory and steering group a considerable development of thought from the time when scientific processes, abstracted from particular scientific contents, were the object of investigation (in keeping with the general aims of the APU) to the present time when what is to be assessed includes 'physical science concepts', and so on. To that extent the APU is suggesting what ought to be the content of the curriculum that should be looked at in any national monitoring as judged by those who know their science.

The science steering group has in consequence produced a map of the territory which, incorporating certain formal qualities of scientific thinking as well as scientific content, would, I suspect, be regarded by most as a valuable contribution to curriculum thinking. But the failure to maintain for assessment purposes the clear division between processes and content is worth reflecting upon. In the early discussions of the working group, the criteria for the science monitoring were to emphasize 'processes' – intellectual and practical skills used in science. These were contrasted with 'the knowledge of chief facts, laws and principles of science'. However, an adequate characterization of the territory came to be seen as much more complex than such a distinction would suggest – just as the oft-quoted distinction between knowledge as process and knowledge as product is, in its simplicity, a distortion of what it means to know. To engage in any enquiry requires the use of concepts. And concepts, though in one sense the product of others' enquiries, become a necessary part of the continuing process of enquiring. Furthermore the concepts themselves, part of the process of enquiring, are logically connected to particular theories. The formal properties of thinking in any area are so intimately bound up with the matter thought about that it is not at all clear how the one can be assessed without the other, not just in the sense that the content is necessary to *illustrate* the formal qualities (the general processes of thinking), and not just in the sense that the content is merely the medium through which these formal qualities can operate, but in the sense that the content enters into the very conception of the processes themselves.

I believe this also to be true of moral development. Morality has a content, and this of course affects profoundly the way in which such development should be assessed. But of course there are many who would disagree, and such disagreement must create problems for any national programme of assessment.

The selection of objectives

The APU aims to provide a picture of pupil performance. It does not aim to prescribe what shall be taught in schools. Hence it is important to produce a framework that itself does not influence the school curriculum but simply provides a means of reporting what in fact happens. It is not of course denied that there will be *some* influence upon the school curriculum but it is felt that this can be kept to an insignificant minimum by the curriculum model adopted. However I have already indicated how, in the adoption of this model, in the focus upon development, and in the failure to maintain the distinction between general processes and specific content, the APU is not in a position simply to reflect what is the case. Indeed this is particularly apparent when it comes to the formulation of the curriculum objectives that are to be assessed.

It might seem possible to reflect what generally is happening in schools by asking teachers – and then basing the programme of monitoring what is happening, and to what degree, on what teachers say is happening. There could, in other words, be a survey of what teachers claim to be doing as a basis for drawing up a 'check list' within each of the different areas.

There are, however, very considerable conceptual problems in proceeding in this way. The connections between what in fact happens and what teachers say is happening are often tenuous. This is due partly to the elasticity of the concepts that people employ to describe teaching and different kinds of development (people use the same words to describe different events, and different words to describe the same event), and partly to the lack of objectivity in most accounts of school and classroom experience. There is not an unambiguous and universally agreed language of educational practice. Furthermore, even if there were agreement in language we would probably find that, within the areas of aesthetics, physical development, and personal and social development, there would be little pupil performance that was universally agreed to be a worthy component of the curriculum. To create instruments of assessment on the basis of what in fact goes on in schools (as though there is empirical backing for this basis and, thus, as though such assessment is not a particular reflection of the priorities of the APU) simply does not make sense. And the consequences of this false claim are dangerous when possibly a major function of APU assessment will be the provision of a base line, from which local authorities might begin their testing of schools and children within their respective areas.

It is interesting to see how the National Assessment of Educational Progress in the USA tried to cope with this particular issue. The formulation of objectives within any particular area underwent a prolonged period of consultation with groups representing teachers, subject specialists, and the wider community. The final list of objectives were those agreed upon both within and between these three groups. On the other hand each group, and then the three groups together, omitted those objectives which may very well have been of central importance to individual schools or groups of schools but which were not generally agreed upon. It is possible, in attempting to reach consensus, to agree only upon those matters that in fact are of fringe interest. The richness of the curriculum, reflected in its variety and the division of teacher opinion, could get neglected.

Where objectives are agreed upon there is of course a grave danger of assessing them by means which are easy to administer and to score. The APU has professed continually that it seeks a variety of ways of assessing performance, and will in no way confine itself to paper and pencil, multi-choice items. Difficulties there will of course be in pursuing such an open policy, not the least of which will be expense. But there is also the danger, especially if the policy is adopted of banking items with a specific technical value, of concentrating upon objective-type questions that can be expressed in precise behavioural terms, and that can be standardized and used to calibrate similar items used in local authority testing.

Conclusion

The APU has embarked upon a programme of monitoring school performance that is a most important element in the general movement towards making schools more accountable. Many aspects of its work – its adoption of light sampling procedures, its conceptual mapping of different curriculum areas, its research into different techniques of assessment and of banking items – have broken new ground and have changed in a significant and, in my view, admirable way what that accountability means. But there are areas of its thinking that remain as yet obscure, and that, if not examined critically, could have serious consequences. I have pointed to four areas of difficulty in the monitoring of pupil performance on a wide scale – that is, in obtaining a broad picture that aims not to be prescriptive. There are obviously others that I have not touched upon – the effect, for example, of choosing particular background variables within which to interpret the results. But my main problem is that one cannot abstract sufficiently from particular curriculum content and programmes of instruction to get an adequate framework for the diversity of curriculum aspiration. Once this is acknowledged, then the role of the APU in curriculum development and the need for more in-depth examination of what happens in schools, will be much more clear.

References

APU (1977) *Assessment of Scientific Development*. London: DES.
—— (1978) *Language Performance*. London: DES.
—— (1979) *Science Progress Report 1977–78*. London: DES.
Bullock Report (1975)*A Language for Life*. London: HMSO.
Damon, W. (1977) *The Social World of the Child*. London: Jossey-Bass.
Hirst, P. H. (1965) Liberal education and the nature of knowledge. In R. D. Archambault *Philosophical Analysis and Education*. London: Routledge & Kegan Paul.
Peters, R. S. (1971) Moral development: a plea for pluralism. In T. Mischel (ed.) *Cognitive Development and Epistemology*. New York: Academic Press.
Phenix, P. H. (1964) *Realms of Meaning*. New York: McGraw-Hill.
Selman (1976) Social-cognitive understanding: a guide to educational and clinical practice. In T. Lickona (ed.) *Moral Development and Behaviour*. New York: Holt, Rinehart & Winston.

8 Limitations of the Rasch model for educational assessment*

Harvey Goldstein

Introduction

Constructors of educational tests have always contended with two major problems. The first arises from the varied aims and methods of teaching, each of which can make out a case for using its own particular test instruments designed to assess its own set of objectives. Thus if we wish to test, say, arithmetical attainment of eight-year-olds we must decide what the test items are meant to be testing and we should choose a range of items which in some sense are 'fair' to all children. For example, if rote arithmetic items were chosen and the test then administered to children who had not been taught arithmetic in this way, the test could be said to 'discriminate' against these children.

The second problem, which really stems from the first, is the relative impermanence of all educational tests. A test which might be acceptable and appropriate at one time will eventually become dated, either because it becomes

*A slightly more technical version of this chapter can be found in Goldstein (1979a), and a mathematical critique of the Rasch model in Goldstein (1980).

My grateful thanks are due to the following who read and commented on an early draft of this chapter: Steve Blinkhorn, Anne Hawkins, Jan-Eric Gustafsson, Raimo Konttinen, Philip Levy and Bob Wood.

too familiar and children are 'taught the test', or because the individual items in the test themselves become outdated and inappropriate. One of the best-known examples of this is in the study of trends in reading standards in England and Wales from 1948 to 1971 (Start and Wells, 1972). This study, using two tests to cover the whole period, found an apparent increase in reading standards up to the mid-1960s followed by no change in average test scores. This result, however, might not have been due to any real changes in reading standards, but rather to a decreasing relevance of the tests over time, owing to changing language use, teaching methods, curricula, etc. For example, the term 'mannequin parade' used in one of the tests may have been familiar in the 1950s but would be much less familiar by 1970 (Burke and Lewis, 1975). Thus, children may have achieved lower test scores than expected because the test itself had become relatively harder, rather than because their attainments had fallen. Such changes in the relevance of tests can occur even over relatively short periods of time, for instance when the advent of cheap electronic technology begins to influence numeracy skills.

This state of affairs can be contrasted with that in the biomedical sciences where measuring instruments do not suffer these problems, at least not to the same degree. For example, a child's height is always measured by effectively the same well-defined instrument at all ages and times. Of course, there may be considerable debate over the usefulness of using such an instrument in the first place, but once that issue has been resolved we tend to find a general agreement about its continued use in a variety of circumstances. This seemingly desirable situation has stimulated a number of those concerned with the construction and use of mental tests to find ways of approaching it, and the controversy over the use of the Rasch model is perhaps best understood in this context, as will be elaborated below.

In the first of the following sections there is an outline of so-called 'latent trait models' of which the Rasch model is but one special case. This is followed by a more detailed explanation of the Rasch model itself, its assumptions and implications. Although these sections are concerned with basically statistical models defined by mathematical equations, the models will be developed in a relatively non-technical fashion, using a sketch of the algebraic details in order to convey the essential ideas. For those readers who wish to pursue some of the technicalities, references are given. Having described the model, the next section discusses some of the important educational consequences of using the Rasch model, and so-called 'item banks' based on it, in order to monitor educational achievement. Its relevance to the requirements of the government's Assessment of Performance Unit (APU) is also examined.

This chapter, perhaps inevitably, is essentially a critical one and I am aware that, arguing against one particular approach, it may appear that I have nothing to replace it. In an attempt to meet this there is a final brief section which suggests some alternatives, not only to the Rasch model but also to some of the more 'traditional' methods of constructing educational tests. Some of the proposals in that section owe much to the ideas of my friend and colleague Professor Bob Wood.

Latent trait models

Probably the best known and most widely used latent trait model is factor analysis and, because of its familiarity, a brief discussion of it will serve to introduce the essential properties of latent trait models.

The factor analysis model assumes that there are one or more underlying and unobservable factors or traits which characterize an individual and determine his or her observed responses. For example, we might suppose that a few basic traits characterize personality and could we but know what they were and measure them, we could determine how they affected an individual's behaviour. Although we cannot actually measure them, it is supposed that we can assemble measurable 'indicators' of them, which in some sense reflect their operation. In the well-known case of the general intelligence factor or IQ, for example, it is possible to measure individual performance on various tasks or items, the responses to which are assumed (or rather defined) to be determined by a set of underlying factors. Of these, general intelligence is regarded as the most important. The essence of such a model can be written down quite simply, and as an example the following equations describe the form of a factor analysis model with three indicators (X, Y, Z) and two factors (G, H).

$$X = a.G + b.H$$
$$Y = c.G + d.H$$
$$Z = e.G + f.H$$

(1)

where a, b, c, d, e, f are the values of the 'coefficients' (or loadings) of the factors G and H. It is the problem of finding the values of these latter quantities towards which the theory of factor analysis is directed. This model says that, for an individual, each measured indicator is simply a weighted sum of his factor values. Thus the weights for the first indicator (X) are the coefficients a, b. The model can also provide estimates of the factors (factor scores) for each individual in the analysis so that the values of G and H, say, can be compared across individuals. In fact the model is written just like a set of multiple regression equations, the main difference being that the factors have unknown values. As it turns out this implies that in order to be able to estimate the values of the coefficients we need to introduce further assumptions. Because of the general arbitrariness of any set of assumptions, and the fact that different sets of assumptions will generally lead to different results, factor analysis tends to be used most often as an exploratory technique which seeks to uncover the existence of possible factors, rather than to provide objective and definitive estimates of the coefficient values or individual factor values. It is worth noting that, in the special case where it is assumed that only one factor operates, then the coefficients a, c, e can all be estimated without introducing further assumptions. In practice it is rarely assumed that one and only one factor operates, and this point will be pursued later.

It is now a matter of history how some of the earlier advocates of factor analysis in the area of intelligence testing exaggerated its claims, especially with respect to 11-plus selection tests. In large measure these exaggerations and the eventual reactions to them can be traced to a failure to recognize the limitations of the factor analysis model described above and to an attempt to attribute a strong objective reality, rather than an exploratory status, to the general intelligence factor. Thus an interesting research tool achieved an unwarranted use as an 'objective' instrument in the educational classification and selection of children.

Equations similar to (1) underlie all latent trait models. In these, a set of indicators which may be, for example, total test scores or, as in the case of the Rasch model, responses to individual items, is related to a set of unobservable factors or traits. The principal differences lie in the form in which factors are combined together and related to observed values, and in the way in which factors are assumed to be measurable, for example as continuous variables or as categories. Nevertheless, the above remarks about the various limitations of the factor analysis model apply in general to other latent trait models.

The Rasch model

The Rasch model, which is described in Professor Lawton's introductory chapter, can be written as the following simple equation:

$$\log \left\{\frac{P}{1-P}\right\} = b + c$$

(2)

where P is the probability of an individual responding correctly to an item, b is the 'ability' of that individual and c is the 'difficulty' of that item.

A number of points arise from this equation. First, of course, the values of b and c are not directly observable and we have to use the data provided by the pattern of passes and failures for a group of individuals responding to a set of test items in order to obtain estimates of them. Also, as in the case of factor analysis with just one factor, we can obtain such estimates without any further assumptions. Nevertheless, several assumptions have already been made. The first, and most obvious one, is that only one term or quantity (b) is necessary to characterize an individual, or to put it another way, an individual's ability is 'unidimensional'. Likewise, every item has only one characteristic, its difficulty. Although various methods have been suggested for testing the assumption of 'unidimensionality' of difficulty, there has been little work on the problem of adequately testing the 'unidimensionality' of ability. Indeed, the usual methods of testing unidimensionality of difficulty are based essentially *on the assumption* of the unidimensionality of ability. Thus, given that a unidimensional ability is always assumed in the analysis of the model, in order to satisfy or 'fit' the model, the items used must also relate only to one underlying dimension of ability. This immediately differentiates the Rasch model from the usual factor analysis model in which the dimensionality or number of factors is studied in the analysis itself. For example, in testing mathematics, if we believe that children's responses to geometrical items are determined by different mental processes from their responses to algebraic items, then we should not be using both types in a model such as (2). This unidimensionability assumption is therefore a stringent one since it must govern our choice of items at the outset. Thus, if we do not take care judiciously to select items, then the model may well not fit the data and, although it may be possible to force a fit and to achieve a single dimension by allowing the analysis to remove 'discrepant' items, there is no guarantee that any sensible interpretation can be placed on the end product. The second point to notice about equation (2) is that the relative difficulty of the items in a test is the same for all individuals. This is the second strong assumption made by the model, although it is perfectly possible to have models which are unidimensional in ability which do not require this assumption. Hence, if we were satisfied that a test tapped only one dimension of ability, in order to use the Rasch model we would also require that, despite experiences, learning sequences, etc., the difficulty order of items was the same for every individual.

The third point concerns what is known as the 'local independence' assumption. This says that, for any individual, the response to an item is completely independent of his or her response to any other item. This again makes strong assumptions which can be violated in a number of ways.

For a technical discussion of some aspects of the issues raised in this section the reader is referred to Lord and Novick (1968).

In view of the strong assumptions made by the Rasch model, it might be thought that serious effort would have been applied to developing tests for them. This seems not to have occurred and until it does we are left with an inadequate basis for fully testing the Rasch model. Certainly, in any large programme to evaluate the Rasch model it will be important to compare the results of analysing samples with very different characteristics. We should, for example, apply the model to minority groups, disadvantaged children, etc. in order to see whether the same item difficulty values are found in every case. This again does not seem to have been undertaken to any extent in any field of education and, until it is, we will not be justified in claiming much generality for the model. In this context it is interesting to note, as Denis Lawton points out, that the APU was originally linked closely to the government's Educational Disadvantage Unit.

To conclude this section I would like to mention a philosophical issue which has arisen in the debate over the Rasch model. Among others, Willmott and Fowles (1974) make the following statement: 'The criterion [of the adequacy of the model] is that items should fit the model, and not that the model should fit the items.' Their emphasis, in other words, is on defining a test *in order that it fits the Rasch model*. Thus the techniques they use for deciding upon the adequacy of the model are seen not as indicating that the model itself possibly might not apply, but rather as tools for rejecting those items of a test which behave differently from the core of items which do conform to the Rasch model. Hence the attainment which is being assessed is effectively defined by those items which happen to conform to the Rasch model. As was pointed out in the previous section, such a procedure holds no guarantee that the results will have a real life interpretation. The implications of such a philosophy, which chooses its test content primarily on statistical rather than educational grounds, is examined in the next section.

Implications of using the Rasch model for educational assessment

It will be useful to consider a particular educational area to illustrate how the Rasch model might work in practice.

Consider testing the arithmetic attainment of a national sample of ten-year-olds. First of all, it will be recognized that in devising a fair test we are not measuring solely an 'inherent' ability to do arithmetic, but rather the accumulated experience of each child. This will encompass the curricula he has been exposed to, the type of teaching he has received, his social background, etc., as well as anything one might think of as 'native ability' in the subject; a situation, as explained below, where we might expect the Rasch model to fail.

Suppose it were possible, however, for the sake of argument, to eliminate the comparative effects of differing curricula etc., for example by selecting a very homogeneous group of children. Would we now expect the Rasch model to provide a reasonable description of the responses to a suitable set of test items? Would we, for example, expect items to appear in the same order of difficulty for all children? The answer will depend on which items are used. It might be possible to select items which did fit the model, but it is by no means clear that this is the kind of test we would want to construct; unless, that is, we were to adopt seriously the philosophy referred to at the end of the last section. Indeed, Wood (1978) has shown how a series of purely random events can produce an excellent fit to the Rasch model, so that the existence of a well-fitting set of items does not necessarily mean that they are measuring anything meaningful. The items of the arithmetic test which fitted the model might reflect, for example, the same common response of the children to the education they had all been exposed to, whereas our real interest might be in those items which did *not* appear to have the same difficulty for all the children. Of course, this immediately raises the problem of how we should choose and then combine a set of items into a single measure of arithmetic attainment, and this point will be taken up in the final section. For now it is sufficient to point out that, even if we could construct a well-fitting Rasch model in a situation where we might expect this to be possible, there is still no necessary educational reason for preferring it over any other method of test construction.

The above arguments do not necessarily imply, of course, that the Rasch model may not be of considerable use outside the area of educational testing. Psychologists, for example, are often concerned to attempt to isolate unidimensional mental traits and the Rasch model may have an important exploratory role to play here. It is perhaps worth emphasizing, however, that the preoccupations of the psychologist are not identical with those of the educationalist. As pointed out earlier with factor analysis, the adoption of models from the former discipline by the latter is not a straightforward procedure.

Once we leave the above example of the homogeneous group of children and consider the real world, the difficulties of applying the Rasch model multiply, and it seems *a priori* unlikely that, for example, a reasonable and fair set of items can be found which appear in the same difficulty order for all children. Indeed, the essence of many educational systems is the diversity of approaches whose actual aim is to create differential attainments among otherwise similar children, for example by way of the order of teaching or as a result of differential pedagogical objectives. While this situation need not rule out the possibility of a single common assessment, it does seem to be at odds with the rationale underlying the Rasch model.

Some of the above objections to the Rasch model do seem to be acknowledged in Bruce Choppin's chapter, where he accepts that no model will fit a body of data perfectly, since all models make simplifying assumptions. He suggests, nevertheless, that departures from the model (the 'residuals') give valuable information, especially with respect to changes over time. Choppin seems to see this as part of an examination of whether one or more dimensions, and hence presumably Rasch scales, are necessary in order to describe attainment. Even so, this still fails to deal with the effects of different pedagogical objectives etc. which will operate within each of these dimensions of attainment, a point which Graham Tall illustrates using some detailed examples in his chapter. Moreover, it is reasonable to expect that directly useful information will be contained in the departures only if the original model is itself valid. If, say, a quite unreasonable model were to be fitted to a set of data, then the departures should indicate the inadequacy of the model itself, rather than yielding 'detailed and valuable information about the objects under study'.

Item banks, the Assessment of Performance Unit and trends over time

If the Rasch model actually worked in education, with a large set of items, and applicable to all individuals in a particular subject area, then in principle we could determine the difficulty value of every item and store these in a 'bank' for future use (for a description of such a proposed bank in mathematics see Purushothaman (1976)). Thus a test could be constructed using any selection of the items suitably covering the range of ability expected in the subjects to whom it will be given. Since the difficulty values of the items are known, the 'difficulty' of the test is known, and an individual's ability is found simply by counting the number of correct responses or passes and then referring this score to a calibration table compiled for the particular test, which converts this score to an ability value on the common underlying scale. Thus, a detailed system of tailor-made tests could be constructed, suitable for children following different curricula without the need for extensive standardization. Moreover, there would also be absolute comparability over time since new, and more relevant, items could be calibrated and incorporated in the bank and out-of-date items dropped, with a common reference scale for all the remaining items.

So much for the dream. The educational reality, as argued above and elsewhere (Goldstein and Blinkhorn, 1977), is altogether different and has to do with a world which is too rich and complex to be reduced, without distortion, to such a simple model. Even so, and despite this, there is an inherent flaw in the item bank concept which would make it unworkable in practice. If we suppose that each of the items in the bank has a prescribed difficulty value, then it is strictly meaningless within the context of the Rasch model to speak of one item as being *more applicable* to one point in time rather than another. The only meaning which can be attached to such a statement must be in terms of difficulty values. For example, suppose we have two items, one of which is more applicable in 1975 than 1980 and the other which is more applicable in 1980 than 1975. Then these two items will have different relative difficulties in the two years and indeed their relative difficulty might become reversed between 1975 and 1980. Hence, by definition, they cannot belong to a single common Rasch scale extending over the five-year period 1975–1980. Nor is it possible to 'calibrate' their difficulties via other items, whose difficulties, for the sake of argument, are assumed to remain constant. Thus an item bank which is designed so that out-of-date items can be replaced is a strictly non-Raschian concept. Similar logic applies to the so-called 'tailored testing' procedures mentioned above, where it is claimed that items can be selected from an item bank to suit different curricula. Since a major justification for the use of the Rasch model is the construction of item banks for just the above purposes, it is unclear what role this model might have once we accept that these purposes are unattainable.

Turning now to the Assessment of Performance Unit (APU) of the Department of Education and Science (DES), we find that one of the principal aims of its monitoring programme is to compare educational attainments over time. It was originally proposed that this could be achieved by utilizing an item bank based on the Rasch model (Kay, 1976). Not only can the Rasch model not fulfil this aim, there is no other simple procedure which will do so either. As pointed out in the first section, there is no absolute basis on which the comparisons can be made over time. This seems to be a fact of life and we really ought to accept it with good grace and try to discover precisely what we *can* usefully say about changes over time. In the following final section I shall outline briefly an alternative direction in which we might profitably turn our attention.

Alternatives to Rasch

The above critique of latent trait models, and especially the Rasch model, starts from the assumption that the criteria which properly ought to determine the content of an educational test are primarily educational rather than statistical. Phrased in this way, perhaps few would disagree. In recent years, the idea of a predominantly educational motivation for test content has found one expression in the development of so-called criterion-referenced tests. These abandon traditional test construction procedures in favour of tests composed of items each of which is designed to assess an articulated educational aim. As they are normally employed, the tests simply report whether or not each student achieves these aims (or passes the items) and comparisons *between* students are avoided and population norms are not used. Nevertheless, it is perfectly possible to calculate population norms and to compare students using these tests. Indeed, not to do so is to impose an artificial and unnecessary restriction, and the most important aspect of criterion-referenced testing is its emphasis on the assessment of specific educational objectives. This point will be elaborated below, following a brief comment on traditional test construction techniques.

Two of the more important concepts traditionally used in the construction of mental tests are that the items comprising the test should be as 'homogeneous' as possible, and that the test itself would have a high 'reliability'. The homogeneity criterion means that the items are all measuring 'the same thing', and here we meet again the idea of a single underlying dimension around which the test is constructed. The procedures for obtaining homogeneity, however, are less stringent than in the case of the Rasch model and the increased flexibility allows more scope for the operation of educational criteria. All the same, there is still the assumption that an educational test should be measuring only one underlying dimension. Wright (1977) puts the point in an extreme form: 'if they do not [bear on a single common latent variable], then the set of items contains a mixture of variables and there is no simple, efficient or unique way to know their utility for measuring anything.'

The reliability concept says that the test score should have a high stability. In a proper test–retest situation an individual's score should not change markedly in relation to the total variability in scores between all individuals in the population. That is, there should be small 'measurement error'. Such a requirement is common to all kinds of measurements and is not one which in any way conflicts with educational content criteria.

If, now, we allow ourselves to move from the doctrine of a single underlying trait, we can allow educational criteria properly to determine test content. We may decide, for example, that a test of arithmetic should consist of an equal number of 'new' maths and 'traditional' maths items, with equal weight being given to each item in computing the overall test score. There will almost certainly be more than one 'dimension' present in such a test. We might alternatively decide to give relatively greater weight to each of the 'new' maths items (or alternatively include more of them) on the grounds that these are thought to be more important educationally. Yet again, we might determine the relative item weightings in such a way that the total test score was the best predictor of, say, later achievement in a group of children. No one of these approaches could be said, *a priori*, to be universally superior to the others. Each will be appropriate in a different context and relevant to answering different types of questions. Incidentally, the fact that an equal item weighting system happens to be the way in which an ability score is computed if we use the Rasch model does not mean that we are, therefore, necessarily using the Rasch model just because we use equal item weightings in a test. Thus, Wright (1977) claims too much when he asserts that anyone who uses a system of equal weighting 'is assuming that their items are in fact working in just the way modelled by Rasch, whether they realise and capitalise on that assumption or not'. Choppin (*Q.V.*) produces a similar statement.

If we decide to construct tests as described in the previous paragraph this does not mean that we can abandon other criteria for deciding what are good items to use. We would still wish to have a high reliability and, at least for measurement purposes, we should not want to include poorly discriminating items, for example items that all the subjects can pass easily. We also need to pilot any new test, and we certainly need good random samples on which to standardize it. The kind of test referred to in the previous paragraph can be likened to what is found in most public examinations which attempt to cover one or more syllabuses with a representative and fair set of questions. It is also found in other areas, for example the Retail Price Index is based on a collection of separate indicators or items. While there may be disagreements on particular items or weightings, there is still a consensus that the index is a useful thing to have. Perhaps this is how we should come to think of educational attainment tests. Also, in addition to reporting test scores we might wish to report, say, the detailed pass rates of individual items or small clusters of cognate items, rather like the National Assessment of Education Performance (NAEP) in the US.

The above emphasis on the qualitative element in educational test construction seems to have several advantages. It focuses attention on where it belongs – the educational aims being assessed – and focuses any conflict of aims at a crucial point, namely when the measuring instrument itself is being constructed. Naturally, with such measuring instruments test constructors and users will have to forgo the luxury of having absolute comparisons over time and instead will have to think, for example, of comparisons between groups of subjects at different times, using tests appropriate to each. For example, if interest lay in regional differences in arithmetic at two points in time, we might well wish to make comparisons on the basis of different tests, each one appropriate to the epoch referred to. If it was felt that, in 1980, an arithmetic test should attach less importance to mental arithmetic skills than one which was administered in 1950, then the more useful regional comparisons will be those which compare regional differences using the test given in 1950 with those differences found using a separate but appropriate test in 1980. Indeed, in the case of the reading tests discussed earlier, an attempt to provide absolute comparisons has tended simply to result in inappropriate and out-of-date measuring instruments with a limited utility. (A more detailed discussion of comparisons across time is given in Goldstein, 1979b, 1981.)

In summary, I am arguing for a shift of emphasis away from a concern with the development of mathematical models aiming at neat technical solutions, and towards a development of quantitative assessment techniques which are firmly rooted in qualitative educational objectives.

References

Anderson, E. B. (1977) Sufficient statistics and latent trait models. *Psychometrika* **42**, 69–81.

Burke, E. & Lewis, D.G. (1975) Standards of reading: a critical review of some recent studies. *Educ. Res.* **17**, 163–74.

Goldstein, H. (1979a) Consequences of using the Rasch Model for educational assessment. *Brit. Educ. Res. J.* **5**, 211–20.

—— (1979b) Changing educational standards: a fruitless search. *J. of National Assoc. of Inspectors and Educational Advisers*, Autumn 1979 **11**, 18–19.

—— (1980) Dimensionality, bias, independence and measurement scale problems in latent trait test score models. *Brit. J. Math. and Statist. Psychol.* **32**, 234–46.

—— (1981) Measuring trends in test performance over time. Paper given to Assessment of Performance Unit seminar, 23 June.

—— & Blinkhorn, S. (1977) Monitoring educational standards – an inappropriate model. *Bull. Br. Psychol. Soc.* **30**, 309–11.

Kay, B. (1976) Justified impatience. *The Times Educational Supplement*, 1 October 1976.

Lord, F. M. & Novick, M. R. (1968) Statistical theories of mental test scores. Reading, Mass.: Addison-Wesley.

Purushothaman, M. (1976) *Secondary Mathematics Item Bank*. Slough: NFER.

Rasch, G. (1960) *Probabilistic Models for Some Intelligence and Attainment Tests*. Copenhagen: Danmarks Paedagogiske Institut.

Start, K. B. & Wells, B. K. (1972) *The Trend of Reading Standards*. Slough: NFER.

Willmott, A. S. & Fowles, D. E. (1974) *The Objective Interpretation of Test Performance*. Slough: NFER.

Wood, R. (1978) Fitting the Rasch Model: a heady tale. *Br. J. Math. Statist. Psychol.* **31**, 27–32.

Wright, B. D. (1977) Misunderstanding the Rasch Model. *J. Educ. Measurement* **14**, 219–25.

9 The possible dangers of applying the Rasch model to school examinations and standardized tests*

Graham Tall

The desire for accurate educational measurement and the search for means of comparing educational standards have long been with us; as a government White Paper stated in 1978:

> The importance of keeping standards as similar as possible is widely recognised by those concerned with public examinations. The examining boards and the Schools Council (1) have a continuing programme of work designed to ensure the maximum comparability of standards as represented by examination grades. (HMSO, 1978)

The relationship between examinations and the curriculum is widely recognized by those involved in education. It is not accidental that the Nuffield 'O' and 'A' level science projects, the Schools Council Integrated Science Project (SCISP), the Sixth Form Mathematics Project

*This paper was first presented at a joint seminar between the Schools Council and the London Institute of Education on 24 October 1978. In formulating my views I have been helped by comments from members of the Schools Council Research Team, Professor H. Goldstein of the London Institute of Education and Mr P. Bush of the Scottish Certificate Examining Board.

(Maths Applicable), Geography for the Young School Leaver and the History 13–16 project all worked closely with examination boards to devise examinations which tested the curriculum as *they wished it to be taught*. By contrast, the link between standardized tests and the curriculum has largely gone by default. Teachers rarely see the tests used by employers to assess their pupils, and employers often fail to recognize that tests which once employed questions similar to those used in schools are no longer, if they ever were, relevant to measure a candidate's potential as an employee or the extent to which he has mastered particular skills and concepts (2).

In an era when so much emphasis is placed on 'objectivity', 'comparability', 'maintenance of standards' (see Lawton's introduction), and test/examination performance it is hardly surprising that the Rasch model which is purported to provide 'objective' data (3) and solve problems of comparability etc. should receive so much attention and support. Within the NFER the number of researchers recommending its use (Choppin (1977), Willmott and Fowles (1974), Dobby and Duckworth (1979)) suggests that the model could be used to develop the next generation of standardized tests, attempts to measure standards of attainment within some areas of the APU as well as in curriculum development. Logically, too, it should be of interest to the examination boards (4) who already find it valuable to store multiple choice items and to collect data which enable considered judgements to be made on whether to retain, improve or reject individual questions.

If the various claims made for the Rasch model by Choppin (1977) and others are valid, it would appear that by the simple expedient of drawing some of the questions from the same bank, examination boards could compare the relative difficulty of two examinations even if the examinations had no questions in common, and curriculum developers would be able to compare the merits of two conflicting teaching approaches. If the model really is in danger of becoming 'the philosopher's stone of the psychometricians' (Goldstein and Blinkhorn, 1977) then it is essential that teachers and others concerned with the curriculum should debate seriously whether the model's proposed advantages are valid, and if so, whether they outweigh its disadvantages if any. To evaluate this, it is necessary first to consider how a Rasch item bank is produced.

The process of setting up the bank is both relatively cheap and straightforward. Items selected by a panel of subject experts are presented in various combinations to different groups of students. The difficulty level of each item is then calculated for each group of students. Only those items maintaining their relative difficulty level across the groups are used in creating the bank. It is essential to note that items are rejected on statistical grounds even if, to subject experts, they continue to appear to be measuring skills or concepts highly relevant to ultimate success in the subject under study. Because the items retained maintained their relative difficulty level, it is assumed that:

1 the relative level of difficulty will continue to remain constant over time;

2 the relative level of difficulty will stay the same even though the learning experiences and the groups of pupils differ;

3 the results of pupils tested on any one combination of items can be directly compared with pupils tested on any other combination of items drawn from the same bank.

For those involved in education to accept the above assumptions requires a considerable act of faith in a model which considers only two factors, item difficulty and individual ability, in assessing the probability of a student getting a particular item correct. The requirement for an act of faith is self-evident; however much effort is spent in creating an item bank it cannot test concepts not yet taught or teaching approaches not yet used in schools.

As the remainder of this paper is primarily concerned to demonstrate, use of the model is self-justifying. The process used to create the Rasch item bank serves to reject items which are affected by different teaching approaches. The claims made on its behalf for comparability over time will help to create a climate of opinion in favour of the status quo with respect to teaching approach and curriculum development. Put simply, as I hope to demonstrate below, the model is in educational terms unbelievably naive; unfortunately it is equally seductive.

The effect of different teaching methods

Curriculum developers clearly believe that they can enhance pupil learning and teach concepts previously thought too difficult by changing or refining teaching methods. This can be illustrated by reference to two examples drawn from the teaching of subtraction. These have been chosen because possible results of their use can be described in concrete terms. In non-numerical examples the differences will still occur though they may be less immediately devious.

In Example 1, pupils using method (c) would be expected to be both more accurate and slower than pupils using methods (a) or (b). This means that in a timed test involving twenty problems a pupil using method (c) might answer only the first ten, but get them all correct, whilst a pupil using method (a) or (b) might attempt eighteen or nineteen questions, failing on several but still getting ten or more correct. The effect this will have on the difficulty level of the various questions is quite clear. The first ten questions will appear to be 'easier' for the first pupil than for the second, whilst the second set of questions would appear to be more difficult. In the extreme situation the difficulty level of items presented to two such groups of pupils might be quite disparate. In fairness to

Rasch, assuming that the test items are all equivalent, the major problem here is common to all timed assessments, that accuracy may be subservient to speed.

A much greater weakness is the Rasch assumption that items in an item bank will retain their relative order of difficulty irrespective of the particular teaching method used. The validity of this assumption depends upon the naive belief that the order of difficulty of the questions in an item bank reflects the difficulty of the concept and that this is identical for different teaching methods; experience shows that this is not the case:

1   The introduction of a new method of introducing subtraction, such as 'matching' or the 'line' method could, as illustrated in example 2, completely transform pupils' concepts of negative numbers, making questions involving them inevitably easier. Indeed many concepts once considered too difficult for pupils to comprehend are now commonly taught. It is commonplace that what is PhD work now will, in the future, be in the sixth form and even lower school syllabus in the future. In schools Bruner's (1960) hypothesis has in practice received considerable support.

2   Teaching methods can be biased solely towards improving examination performance with the result that pupils' attainments appear to rise even though in practice they fall as far as the pupils' whole development is concerned. This would happen in a scientific subject with no practical examination if the teacher reduced the amount of practical work and used the time 'saved' to improve examination technique and to go through old examination papers.

There remains a real danger that the Rasch model, by apparently providing an 'objective' measure, will inhibit new developments. No examination can pick up all the values inherent in a new teaching approach, indeed it is commonly found, when new methods are introduced, that pupils taught by them achieve relatively disappointing results on old-style examinations. To a large extent this is because examinations reflect (produce?) the predominant teaching style found in schools and hence are biased against new methods which may be equally effective in teaching the basic concepts involved, though not in answering the particular questions asked. Thus, if an item bank to test the level of arithmetical understanding of pupils in junior schools had been created at a time when the majority of pupils were taught subtraction using 'take away' (see Example 2) then questions involving negative numbers would probably have been rejected either because the teachers involved considered they were too difficult or because they failed to fit the model – too difficult or having inconsistent difficulty levels with respect to other items in the bank. It is probable, therefore, that the over-precise approach involved in the production of an item bank would even further tip the balance against new teaching methods by causing rejection of the questions where they are superior to traditional methods. Why waste time on new teaching methods which have no opportunity to show their strengths and which tend to reduce the time available for traditional preparation?

Example 1

Five methods are given below. Method (a) is the one used by most adults. Method (b) is preferred by a number of teachers. Method (c) appears to be slower and more cumbersome, but has the real advantage that it can be used effectively with less able pupils by avoiding subtraction (N.B. because of its simplicity and accuracy it is the usual method of calculating the amount of change to give in a shop). Method (d) is illustrative of methods which have some appeal but are not yet widely used in schools, whilst the fifth is a pupil's description of his own method. This latter was described by McIntosh (1978) in an unpublished article, the figures have been changed to make the example consistent.

Sum	365−
	178
Answer	187

Method (a) *Equal additions*

$$3 \rceil^1 6 \rceil^1 5 \qquad \text{or} \qquad (\ \ 3)(\ 16)(\ 15)$$
$$2 \rfloor \ 8 \rfloor \ 8 \qquad\qquad\qquad (\ -2)(\ -8)(\ -8)$$

1	8	7		1	8	7

Method (b) *Decomposition*

$$2 \ \ 5 \rceil^1 5 \qquad \text{or} \qquad (\ 200) + (\ 150) + (\ 15)$$
$$1 \ \ 7 \ \ 8 \qquad\qquad\qquad (-100) + (\ -70) + (\ -8)$$

1	8	7		100 +	80 +	7

Method (c) *Additive*

178 to 180 is   2+
180 to 200 is 20
200 to 300 is 100
300 to 365 is 65
                    ___
                    187
                    ___

Method (d) This does not involve 'carrying', instead the hundreds, tens and units subtractions are carried out separately as follows (look carefully at the actual subtraction!):

$$
\begin{array}{r}
300 \\
-100 \\
\hline
200
\end{array} \quad + \quad 200
$$

$$
\begin{array}{r}
70 \\
-60 \\
\hline
-10
\end{array} \quad - \quad 10
$$

$$
\begin{array}{r}
200 \\
- 10 \\
\hline
190
\end{array}
$$

$$
\begin{array}{r}
8 \\
-5 \\
\hline
3
\end{array} \quad - \quad 3
$$

$$
\begin{array}{r}
- 3 \\
\hline
187
\end{array}
$$

Method (e) *An eleven-year-old pupil's method*:

'I decided to take the hundred away first. That was two hundred. I forgot those and rounded off the other numbers to the next ten upwards. Eighty from two hundred is one hundred and twenty. Discard the hundreds and keep the twenty. Now, because the eighty you took was really seventy-eight, add a two and the five from the sixty and then put them all together with the sixty. That makes eighty-seven. Now add the hundreds and you get one hundred and eighty-seven.'

Example 2

Three of the commonest methods of introducing the concept of subtraction are 'take away', 'matching' and the 'line method'. Inevitably all have advantages and disadvantages and may be used in combination. In the hands of teachers with a poor mathematical background there remains real danger to the concept of negative numbers, see below:

(a) *Take away*   8 − 3 = 5

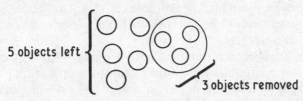

5 objects left

3 objects removed

Pupil: 'Eight objects take away three leaves five'. If badly presented this can create the concept in a pupil's mind that: 'Five take away eight can't be done'.

(b) *Matching*   8 − 3 = 5

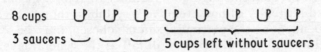

8 cups

3 saucers

5 cups left without saucers

Pupil: 'Three cups have saucers, but five do not'. An alert teacher can use this method to indicate not only that there are five spare cups (+5) but also that there are five saucers short (−5).

$$\text{i.e. } 8 - 3 = +5$$

$$\text{and } 3 - 8 = -5$$

(c) *Line method*   8 − 3 = 5

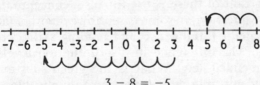

3 − 8 = −5

The effect of a change in syllabus content or emphasis on the relevance of a Rasch item bank

It is widely recognized that new examination syllabuses have an automatic and dramatic effect on the teachers involved. The recent proposals of the JMB board, for example, to increase the mathematical content in subjects like geography, had a measurable effect on the willingness of geography teachers to work with a group of mathematicians in Manchester.

New topics cause teachers both anxiety with respect to their own capabilities and additional preparation. The extent to which the teacher is aware of new developments in his field and understands the concerns of the examiners are major factors affecting his pupils' success in the initial years of a new system. Teachers who can provide accurate information on, and an interesting approach to, new materials make it easier for their pupils to understand and learn the concepts involved. Initially therefore, the measured difficulty of new items in a syllabus, though highly dependent on the particular sample chosen, must be over-estimated. Item difficulty will fall as the general level of expertise increases, again making comparability from year to year impossible. The same phenomenon occurs when new types of examination questions are asked.

The Rasch over-emphasis on general and verbal intelligence

A number of factors inevitably interact to determine the difficulty level of examination/test questions. Ideally the most important of these is the intrinsic conceptual difficulty of the question. In some cases however other factors, notably general intelligence and reading skills, become influential. The difference in discrimination levels between open-ended (e.g. What is the green substance in plants?) and multiple choice questions is explicable on this basis. Whilst it is easy to write one or two good 'distractors' the remaining alternative (s) in multiple choice questions tend to depend for their incorrectness on a very precise use of language. In some multiple choice questions students even need to try and work out which of the answers is more correct (Harper (1978); see also Friel and Johnstone (1978), Leeser (1978), Duckworth and Hoste (1976)).

According to the Rasch model (Choppin, 1977) the difficulty level of all items in a bank should lie within a specified range (5). The danger is that this requirement may force question writers to make the items more difficult using one or more of the methods indicated above. If this occurs then the already present disadvantage of the less intelligent candidate in a test/examination will be increased.

The 'single trait' hypothesis of the Rasch model and its relevance to examinations and employers

Even if the Rasch model was used to produce a new generation of standardized tests the fact that all items in the test are believed to provide measures of the same ability trait would suggest that a whole battery of them would be required to enable the employer to select candidates fairly (see note 2). By contrast, schools examinations are required to reflect the ill-defined nature of their subjects. It is a positive virtue of the system that pupils can achieve identical grades on the same paper by selecting questions which are testing different areas of knowledge and different abilities. Those deeply concerned with ensuring 'comparability' might well disagree with this statement; but they should reflect that the present examination provides pupils, teachers, universities and potential employers with the same single result. Subjects are often very different at 'O', 'A' and degree level; subjects change rapidly over time and the abilities required for success change rapidly too; after obtaining a degree, the specialization required of the graduate may require different talents; all that can be asked of any system requiring such flexibility is that it informs the users of the information that the candidate has achieved a level of success in the particular field. Too many pupils already base their future subject choice on the basis of success in a single examination; any narrowing of the range of abilities leading to success could have quite serious consequences. The effect of using the Rasch model would be inevitably to do just this.

More meaningful examination information

As indicated above, public examinations provide surprisingly little information. If a candidate obtains a grade B in mathematics, for example, it does not mean that he has greater numerical ability than a candidate who obtained a grade C or even D in the same examination. The examination is, after all, concerned with the range of mathematics in the school syllabus and not just with the more limited range of abilities associated with 'number crunching'. Clearly, notwithstanding the comments made above, some more detailed information would be useful in a range of subjects.

Two possible developments are grade examinations, analogous to those used to measure proficiency in music, and profile reports. The former implicitly assumes that subjects are hierarchical in structure and that a series of hurdles could be set up to differentiate between pupils. The latter assumes that the subject can be classified into clearly defined subject areas. Grade levels are much the easiest for users of the information to interpret. A single score indicates whether two pupils are of equivalent ability or, if there is a difference, which of them is superior. Unfortunately, as with the old School Certificate, some pupils will inevitably be disadvantaged due to an asymmetry in their abilities which enables them, for example, to be very competent in algebra but relatively incompetent in more basic mathematical areas such as arithmetic. The lack of a clear hierarchy of concepts in school subjects makes use of the Rasch model particularly dubious.

The problem of difficulty level remains with profile reporting; though, because the areas of knowledge tested are more clearly defined, its effects vary according to the fineness of the classification system used. Unfortunately, the more fine the classification used and hence the more relevant the use of the Rasch model, the greater the length of the test session(s) required, the more overtly complex the interpretation of the results and the potentially more deleterious the effect on the curriculum. Traditionally most subjects have had clearly defined content areas. Thus history was divided by classification based on periods – Elizabethan, Victorian, etc.; mathematics into arithmetic, algebra, geometry and trigonometry; biology into taxonomy, cytology, ecology, etc. In recent years in most, if not all, subjects such classifications have become less acceptable as a way of organizing subject knowledge. Even if the examination system allowed regular reclassification the system would appear to be likely to inhibit learning and the transfer of ideas into other areas of life. It would be positively harmful if such profiles constrained the very real interrelationships which teachers are beginning to develop within and between various parts of the syllabus. Alternatively, classification could be based on (alternative) criteria such as levels of understanding (see SCISP A and SCISP B), but I suspect this would be even harder for the user to interpret let alone the examiner to set.

In summary, the Rasch model is a statistical approach to existing forms of examining which could have a deleterious effect on pupil achievement, choice and curriculum development. The model does not reflect educational reality but produces an over-simplified version which effectively distorts it. It is essential therefore that statements made on its behalf are studied carefully and that glib comments are not allowed to pass unchallenged. Even an *ad hoc* imprecise system which is under constant review is highly preferable to a precise one which purports to measure something that it cannot.

Notes

1   See Schools Council Examination Bulletins and 'Standards in public examinations: problems and possibilities', Comparability in Examinations Occasional Paper 1, Schools Council Forum on Comparability, Schools Council, Autumn 1979.

2   The NIIP tests used by many employers are not con-

cerned with assessing absolute levels of attainment. If the original test questions are deemed too easy then the test writers devise harder questions, and vice versa, in order that the range and distribution of test marks fit the normal distribution. A criterion-referenced test, or test of mastery, is by contrast concerned solely with the extent to which candidates can be said to have mastered skills and concepts on the basis of specific criteria. N.B. The NIIP standardized tests specify a very precise time allowance; Fitzgerald (1979) has demonstrated that making available more time and the opportunity to practice on similar questions raises the overall level of achievement of the candidates and, perhaps even more important, changes considerably the rank order of achievement of the candidates. Finally, relatively few employers seem to check whether the skills they are testing are actually required 'on the job'. Not surprisingly, therefore, the use of such tests may result in the employers doing themselves and the candidates a disservice.

3   Willmott and Fowles (1974) implied that 'objective' means having one value for each pupil. Choppin has compared the measuring ability of a test drawn from a Rasch item bank with that of physical instruments such as a ruler. In using the word objective proponents of the Rasch model appear to be implying more than that the test is objectively marked, has a high content validity (looks right) and reliability (pupil would obtain a similar score on a parallel test), but how much more?

4   Interestingly, the level of interest in the Rasch model by the examination boards appears to be small – a result of their closer links with the educational process?

5   To some extent this is an agreed concept in GCE, but not necessarily CSE, examinations. The difference is that the examination boards are less rigorous with individual items and satisfied as long as the overall distribution of marks achieved allows for a reasonable classification of exam papers into different grades.

References

Bruner, J. S. (1960) *The Process of Education*. New York: Vintage Books.

Choppin, B. (1977) *Item Banking and the Monitoring of Achievement: An Introductory Paper*. Slough: NFER.

Dobby, J. & Duckworth, D. (1979) Objective assessment by means of item banking. Schools Council Examination Bulletin 40. London: Evans/Methuen.

Duckworth, D. & Hoste, R. (1976) Question banking: an approach through biology. Schools Council Examination Bulletin 35. London: Evans/Methuen.

Fitzgerald, A. (1979) Measuring the arithmetical competence of pupils in relation to employment. *Vocational Aspect of Education* 31, 9–21.

Friel, S. & Johnstone, A. H. (1978) A review of the theory of objective testing. *Schools Science Review* 59, 733–8.

Goldstein, H. & Blinkhorn, S. (1977) Monitoring educational standards, an inappropriate model. *Bull. Br. Psychol. Soc.* 30, 309–11.

Harper, G. H. (1978) Standard of question setting in A-level Biology. *School Science Review* 59, 486–91.

HMSO (1978) Government observations on Tenth Report. Cmnd 7124, 5.

Leeser, A. M. (1978) Problems of multiple choice questions. *School Science Review* 60, 158–9.

McIntosh, A. J. (1978) Some subtractions – what do you think you're doing? Unpublished paper.

Willmott, A. S. & Fowles, D. E. (1974) *The Objective Interpretation of Test Performance: The Rasch Model Applied*. Slough: NFER.

10 Educational measurement and the item bank model

Bruce Choppin

Let me begin rather conventionally with some definitions. It is my purpose to convince you that measurement is an operation quite distinct from assessment, examination, evaluation or ranking. From the Oxford Dictionary we have: *to measure* is 'to ascertain the extent or quantity of a thing by comparison with a fixed unit or with an object of known size', or again 'to estimate (an immaterial thing, a person's character, etc.), by some standard or rule', and again from the Random House Dictionary, 'to estimate the relative amount, value, etc. by comparison with some standard'.

In its ordinary everyday usage, *measure* implies quantification, comparison and a certain degree of objectivity and/or standardization. When we deal with 'immaterial things' it can be a demanding process, and one which requires skill and ingenuity. The end product, however, is still a quantification. The view of educational measurement adopted in this paper, simply stated, is that we use *tests* in order to make *measures* of things that are not directly observable, and that these measures subsequently need careful interpretation. The nature of the interpretation, of course, depends upon the purpose for which the measurements were obtained. Measurement is essentially a one-dimensional process. We can speak very generally of size; Bill is bigger than Ben, but if we want to establish this by measurement we have to define the dimension of comparison. Do we mean Bill is taller than Ben, that he weighs more, that he wears larger shoes? On any of these dimensions we can make a measure; on the generalized concept of size, we cannot.

It is possible to distinguish two quite separate schools of thought with regard to educational testing. Misunderstandings which relate to the basic assumptions and approaches to each have led to confusion and controversy – some of it evident in preceding chapters. Each school has adherents in many parts of the world, but in recognition of their geographical origins, I will dub them the Chinese and Danish schools. The Chinese school, to which I suspect some of the other contributors to this volume belong, has a respectable history stretching back some three thousand years. It was in about 1100 B.C. that the Chinese emperors introduced a formal and systematic set of examination procedures for the selection and promotion of civil servants, and ultimately of the Mandarin class that ruled China. Early records of this system, which survived in China until the early years of the twentieth century, are well summarized in Ping-Ti Ho (1962) and DuBois (1968). Here we can readily identify the ancestors of our own university 'finals' and the GCE examinations. The underlying notions are first, that an examination should consist of a sample of tasks designed to elicit responses that more or less represent the behavioural pattern desired in a successful candidate, and second, that the total score on such an examination, however arrived at, is a sound device for ranking candidates and for choosing those who will be able to succeed if selected for higher things. In passing I would draw your attention to the fact that the Chinese examinations usually had pass rates of between one and three per cent, and in these circumstances it is particularly easy to select able candidates even with examinations of rather poor technical quality.

The Danish school is so labelled because of the pioneering work of a Copenhagen mathematician, Georg Rasch, in the 1950s and 1960s. It contains most, if not all, of the prominent latent trait theorists: Andersen, Fischer and Spada from the continent; Wright and Lord from America; and so on. I see myself as belonging to this school, in company with several NFER colleagues, notably Alan Willmott. The prime concern of the Danish school of measurement – and measurement according to the definitions I presented earlier. Most mental tests are made up of a substantial number of separate items. The purpose of an item is to provide a piece of information or evidence which contributes to the measurement which is the object of the test. The reason we have many items is that typically each item contributes only a very small amount of information relevant to achievement on the underlying trait. Members of the Danish school are acutely aware of the severe limitations of mental test items. Such items are not to be compared with the very broad samples of behaviour which occur in other testing situations. I am thinking here of the *driving test* with its typically unpredictable and realistic sample of 'on the road' experiences, the *beam exercises* performed by the Olympic gymnast, or the *performances* offered by musicians in piano, organ or violin competitions. Such complex samples of behaviour permit a generalized and multi-dimensional assessment and evaluation, but scarcely provide an adequate basis for measurement. In mental testing we recognize the limitations of individual items and thus tend to be rather less anxious than others about their content, and their face validity. Items are there in order to measure, and it is their measurement properties of which we take chief note. However, the Danish school's position on this is frequently exaggerated to absurd extremes by members of the Chinese school. The difference is mainly one of emphasis.

In earlier chapters, it is argued that we should allow educational criteria to determine test content. In practice this seems to mean that the construction of tests is dominated by the desire to represent more or less realistically the balance of content, skills and topics found in the appropriate piece of curriculum. Hence it has been argued that educational tests should usually be multi-dimensional – that is that they should be deliberately constructed to stimulate performance on several independent dimensions of attainment. I do not deny that it is possible to construct a test in this way. I ask only what interpretation is to be placed on the total score deriving from such a test. Is the total score a measure? If so in what sense? For what purposes can it be used? Measurement is a *one*-dimensional process. There is a real problem here, and one which item banks can help to solve.

The motivation for an item bank

The underlying logic of item banking has already been developed at length (e.g. Wood and Skurnik (1969), Choppin (1978a)), and I shall not rehearse it here. A great deal of effort is now being invested in the creation of item banking systems and the reader may perhaps be interested in the reasons why, and in a summary of the practical problems involved.

An item banking system is a *measurement system* in that it permits us to make consistent measurements in a wide variety of situations and conditions. Clearly if we only need to make a single measurement under conditions that are essentially fixed, then we do not need the complexity of item banking. A conventional test is sufficient. It may be useful to distinguish the labels *item bank* and *item pool* as they are currently used in the literature. The term *item bank* is reserved for collections of test items organized and catalogued to take into account the content of each test item and also its measurement characteristics (difficulty, reliability, validity, etc.). The characteristics are recorded in such a way that the items can be readily grouped into tests with known psychometric properties, so that the scores from two tests made up of separate sets of items from the bank can be interpreted one in terms of the other. This definition of an item bank excludes a number of collections of test items which have been assembled merely as an aid to the sharing of creative ideas between examiners. The term *item pool* is reserved for any such collection if it lacks the psychometric cataloguing and calibration to permit the type of use described above.

The specific advantages of item banking are:

1 It permits the user to vary the test mode, its length and content, according to local conditions without losing generalizability and consistency of results.

2 It permits the very easy preparation of parallel forms of a test.

3 It offers the possibility of repeated measurements on the same individual on the same dimension without using the same test questions.

4 It permits us to take advantage of the many high-quality test questions that have been composed over the years and to make use of them in a systematic and intelligent way.

In summary, item banking offers psychometric efficiency and above all, user-flexibility when compared to conventional standardized tests. These are important advantages and make up a very strong case for the use of item banks *if* they can be developed.

The central measurement problem

The underlying principle of item banking is that when a user composes tests of items drawn from the bank, the tests so formed will have known measurement characteristics. Most classical test statistics (e.g. reliability, validity, standard error of measurement, mean score) relate to whole tests rather than to individual items. Those that do not (item facility and discrimination index) are strongly sample-dependent, that is, their value is determined by the composition of the sample of people who provided the data on which the item analysis is based. As a rule item banks will not be developed for use only within specified populations of people and so the central measurement problem is to find a way in which to extract statistical information about the measuring properties of individual items from test data free of contamination by the other items that make up the particular test and by the sample of people to which the test was exposed. The subsequent and lesser problem is then to be able to combine these individual item characteristics so as to be able to predict the measurement properties of a new test formed from the bank.

There have been a number of different attempts to tackle this measurement problem and I have space here to consider only three, and then not in much detail. The reader may well wish to go to the original sources for a more adequate description.

Shoemaker

Shoemaker accepts that his item banks may be applied to a wide range of samples and populations which cannot be entirely predicted in advance. He feels however that the domain of items from which his tests will be sampling is fixed and fairly well defined. The items in the bank are taken to be a random sample of those from the entire domain, and the items that make up any particular test are themselves a sub-sample taken from the bank. Shoemaker uses the *proportion correct* score on any test as an estimate of the proportion of items in the bank that could be solved and hence of the proportion of the entire domain that has been mastered. He is, in essence, treating test items from a particular domain as equivalent or interchangeable (Shoemaker, 1975).

Rasch

Rasch's approach proposes that, within a given domain, items do vary on one salient characteristic, that is their difficulty. Rasch formulates an explicit mathematical model for the probability of success on a particular item in terms of a person's ability and the item's difficulty. (In this context, *difficulty* is defined *relative to other items* and not in terms of the rate of success of a *particular group of people* as is the case in conventional norm-referenced item analysis.) He does not deny the possibility of other factors influencing the outcome but proves that the entry of any of these factors in a significant way (e.g. varying discrimination of test items) results in contradictions to the basic principles of 'objective measurement' which demand a unique ordering of item difficulties. Rasch's model is in fact the mathematical base for the conventionally used 'raw score' as a measure on a test, although most users of raw scores remain unaware of this. The Rasch model has been the target of some very strong attacks (Goldstein and Blinkhorn (1977), Wood (1978), Goldstein (1979)), usually on the grounds that its assumptions are untenable. The assumptions, however, are the same as those that underpin conventional item analysis procedures, and in practice Rasch seems to work well wherever conventional test analyses work well (Rasch (1960), Wright (1977)).

Lord

Lord's model differs from the Rasch model in that it makes explicit provision for variations in item discrimination and in a 'guessability' parameter. There is still only a single parameter ability, for the person taking the test. It is argued that this model is closer to real life in that experience has shown that test items do typically differ on more than one dimension. Although mathematically somewhat similar to the Rasch model, Lord's model was developed in a quite different way. The Rasch model was devised from a theoretical set of specifications for 'objective measurement', whereas Lord's model sprang from attempts to explain the behaviour of real items (Lord (1952), Lord (1977).

In practice, item banking seems almost always to be settling for the Rasch model (Choppin, 1978c) or some relatively simple extension of it (e.g. to include non-dichotomous data). It is perhaps worth summarizing briefly why this is so. The chief advantage is undoubtedly that it relies on parameters that are fairly readily estimated from a reasonably small quantity of data. The Lord model on the other hand seems chiefly of academic interest, since almost astronomical quantities of data are required to obtain adequate estimates of the item parameters (there is even some argument as to whether Lord's parameters are properly estimable at all). Shoemaker's model is fairly easy to work with, but suffers from a great disadvantage in that since the items are treated as interchangeable, differences and discrepancies between items cannot really be explored. The Rasch model is convenient in that it produces ability estimates which bear a one-to-one relationship to conventional raw scores. Its ability to answer from a larger set presented, and the fact that it can be extended to handle scoring schemes more complex than 'right/wrong' (such as those which call for partial credit and indeed rating and attitude scales), means that it can be introduced as the basic measuring framework for almost all the types of test material currently in use. There is a price to be paid, of course. Item banks built around the Rasch model have to pay rather more attention to item-validity and good discrimination than do conventional tests, but part of the pay-off for this extra effort comes in the quality of the measuring instruments achieved.

Curriculum considerations

In education we rarely wish to assess student performance on only a single dimension (except in some research applications with which I shall not be much concerned here). Modern ideas of curriculum organization emphasize more and more the integration and interaction of knowledge and skills from different subject areas. There appear to be sound educational reasons for taking a multi-dimensional approach to curriculum. Educational assessment must necessarily be subordinate to and take its priorities from education. It too needs a multi-dimensional approach. Measurement however is a uni-dimensional process, and so, to the extent that educational assessment requires measurement, we have something of a problem.

In my view the answer does not lie in the approach sometimes advocated by members of the GCE Boards and like bodies – that low reliability and lack of objectivity are necessary consequences of going for a vague mixture of traits, elicited by essay or short answer questions, and spanning the range of content in the curriculum. This is unsatisfactory because the score that such an examination produces is not a measurement in any meaningful sense. It is not reproducible, related to external criteria, or interpretable in terms of any psychological constructs. It does offer a basis for ranking pupils – if one closes one's eyes to the largely arbitrary nature of the ordering produced. It does produce a score which generally correlates positively with measures of intelligence – but then so does a measure of height, and this would not generally be held to be a sound method of allocating places in our higher education system. My criticisms of this approach are stronger in those applications wherein the student is asked to choose from a longer list those questions on which he will be assessed (without his being told how the various questions will be marked). This has got a lot in common with betting on horses or greyhounds but little with measurement. The issues involved in assessing complex performance must be faced more directly.

Should we perhaps abandon measurement in education altogether? Some of the reasons advanced for having school examinations (e.g. motivating the student to learn) have almost nothing to do with measurement. Indeed as Skinner has pointed out, a reward and punishment system which includes a random (i.e. chance) element, may in practice be a more efficient conditioning tool than one that does not. Other uses of examinations (e.g. the encouragement of competition through the ranking of students), are viewed by a great many educationists as socially undesirable. If we are going to rank students they might well argue there is no educational advantage in having a precise over an inaccurate measure. On the other hand there do seem to be some valuable roles for educational measurement to play – roles in which the quality of measurement is very important. I will not attempt to give an exhaustive list, but will concentrate on just three of the major ones.

The diagnosis of individual pupil difficulties

Clinical approaches to diagnosis are and always have been time-consuming. Getting to know individual pupils and their learning problems is a major task facing the classroom teacher, and one for which he or she rarely has enough time. Carefully prepared test materials could do a great deal to help by providing objective (albeit limited) information on the problems encountered by individual pupils. Remarkably little has been done in this area in the last fifty years, but item banking would seem to have a lot to offer here. I predict that this will prove to be a growth area in the coming decade.

Curriculum evaluation

This is but one of a number of possible *research* uses where the quality of educational measurement is vital. Despite the writings of various colleagues in Britain and the United States in recent years, I would still contend that an assessment of pupil achievement on cognitive objectives is a necessary part of almost all curriculum evaluations. It has been argued (e.g. Scriven, 1967) that the evaluations required by policy-makers will usually be comparative, and this has caused major problems for test constructors. They have found it difficult to formulate a test that would yield sound and *fair* assessments of achievement for pupils who have followed different curricula with different objectives. Again I must point out that this difficulty results from the use of 'fixed tests'. With a fixed test there is no real solution, but within an item banking system, although the problem does not entirely disappear, it can be adequately solved. For example, it is possible through a careful analysis of elements common to both new and old curricula to develop tests tailored to the needs of each group of pupils, but each scaleable on the same latent trait. This enables direct comparison of the two groups (Engel, 1976). Similar statements could be made about a variety of other research activities in education involving the evaluation of aspects other than curriculum.

Precise educational measurement is important if small changes in performance are to be detected. Studies which employ precise measurement procedures are more likely to yield useful results than those that do not. Further, for any particular change in performance, the sample size needed to yield 'statistical significance' can be reduced, which would normally lead to smaller studies and a consequent saving in cost. These remarks apply even more forcefully in studies of attitude since measures of effective outcomes are often much more unreliable (that is they contain a large component of measurement error) when contrasted with measures of cognitive outcomes.

Monitoring standards of achievement

I do not plan to discuss the APU exercise which has already been dealt with at length. Monitoring standards is now seen as being an essential component of the APU, and it is of course central to various local authority assessment programmes. Currently fashionable assessment models (and this is *not* limited to the Rasch model) depend upon educational measurement, and struggle to cope with the uni-dimensional–multi-dimensional dilemma. With these models, the quality of the measuring instruments is crucial for successful monitoring. The early experiences of NAEP (the National Assessment of Educational Progress) in the United States (Greenbaum *et al.*, 1977) show the dangers of neglecting measurement issues.

Applications of item banks

If it is agreed that we need educational measurement so we have still to consider how it can be achieved through item banking, given that it is essentially a one-dimensional process that we need to apply in what is essentially a multi-dimensional situation. There are at least two approaches, both with strengths and weaknesses. Both are being tried at the moment and it is too early to say which will prove to be the stronger. Fortunately they are not incompatible and so for the time being we can afford to have both.

The first approach would be to work with profiles rather than simple scores. An item bank would in fact be a composite with many component sub-banks each of which contained sets of items measuring single uni-dimensional traits. For example one sub-bank in 'arithmetic' might be concerned with skills in *adding whole numbers*, another with *subtracting whole numbers*, another with *adding vulgar fractions*, and so on. Tests would be constructed from the bank to yield a profile of performance scores.

Assessment of patterns of growth or change would be accomplished through appropriate multivariate statistical techniques. From a measurement point of view this approach is attractive. It offers the potential of extremely fine discriminations between different patterns of performance and may be sensitive to relatively small differences in learning. There are problems to overcome, however. First the educational public would have to be persuaded to use profiles rather than single scores in a routine fashion – something that has never happened in the past. Then there is a certain vagueness as to the definition of the traits to be measured separately. Would the list be regarded as fixed or would it change from time to time? Who would decide when another trait was needed or when an existing one was not essential? Finally, the scale of work necessary to create this style of item bank is enormous. The requirements for writing and pre-testing the items may alone render it impracticable. The NFER is trying to see if it can be done (Dobby and Duckworth, 1979).

The second approach, and the one which I tend to prefer, makes explicit use of deviations from the simple measurement model. If for example we take a mathematics item bank and a single item which relates to some topic in algebra, then responses to the item are interpreted as providing information about the general level of performance in mathematics (that part of the data that fits a single factor measurement model), and also information about the way in which performance on this topic deviates from the overall performance (residual data not fitting the measurement model).

To make progress with this data we must be clear as to the nature of the measurement model we have introduced. It is a model, no more and no less. It is a grossly simplified description of reality. Models are not to be viewed as true or false; they are adequate or inadequate as approximations to reality. This principle applies to all measurement models. A wooden ruler provides a straightforward example of a model for measuring length which, in everyday use, ignores the fact that the distance between the calibrating marks on the ruler varies according to temperature, humidity, tension, etc., as well as that the calibrations were not drawn with perfect precision and the degree of inaccuracy thereby introduced is unknown. The essence of models is that they do not *exactly* portray real situations. They make simplifying assumptions and hence cannot 'fit the data'. The residuals are often treated as random error and ignored. Such is usually the case with the ruler for measuring length, for Newton's laws of motion, for Van der Waal's equation, and for navigation rules based on spherical geometry. It is also the case in the approach to item banking by way of single traits and profiles as outlined above. In general we treat a model as adequate if the residuals from the model are small enough in practice that we feel they can be safely ignored.

Alternatively, residuals can be analysed and interpreted, can perhaps be made to fit another model, and may even lead the way forward to a more comprehensive and satisfactory modelling of the entire process. We know that mathematics achievement is *not* a uni-dimensional trait. We know that there is *neither* a unique ordering of item difficulties for all students, *nor* a unique ordering of student abilities for all items, but this, despite Professor Goldstein's comments, is not a reason for abandoning the Rasch model. Showing that residuals from the model are too large to be ignored is also not sufficient reason to abandon the approach. Residual information can be analysed and can be shown to yield detailed and valuable information about the objects under study. Examples of this may be found in Choppin (1978a) and Engel (1976), but by far the most detailed and thorough exploration of the approach so far can be found in Mead (1976).

If this approach is applied to the assessment of performance in mathematics, for example, then every item in the item bank will be calibrated in terms of its difficulty considered as an indicator of achievement in general mathematics, and also as regards the information it carries in terms of its deviation in a particular direction. An achievement test composed of items from a mix of different topics will yield an overall measure of mathematics achievement (this variable being defined by the sum of the items and their calibrations in the bank) and other information relating to 'discrepancies'. Performance on the co-ordinate geometry items, when gathered together, provides an indication (even a measure) of the extent to which performance in co-ordinate geometry departs from overall performance. Similarly other groupings of items with common elements provide evidence of achievement on other dimensions. I have argued elsewhere (Choppin, 1978b) that this approach provides a far more satisfactory method of monitoring changes over time than does the dependence on individual item facilities such as are reported by the National Assessment of Educational Progress in the United States. With this method, the consumer has to deduce overall changes of performance from evidence that states that 'while 57 per cent of 13 year olds responded correctly to a particular item in 1976, only 52 per cent answered the same item correctly in 1979'. How does the reader judge whether the item is representative of the full test battery, and whether its relevance to the broad curriculum has remained unchanged over the three-year period?

A better way is to rely on more general measures, such as derive from a latent trait analysis, and to use individual items only as a way of illustrating *what* is being measured. We would view mathematics achievement as being represented by the items in the item bank being strung out in multi-dimensional space in a cigar-like shape. The major axis of the cigar is 'school mathematics achievement'. The other axes represent the multi-dimensional nature of mathematics as currently taught in schools. All we know about the nature of school mathematics is contained in the relative difficulties of all the different pairs of items that make up the item bank, and it is of course the sum of all these comparisons that gives us this hypothetical cigar. Over time we anticipate that the shape will change; both the direction of the major axis (i.e. the definition of the underlying 'schools mathematics achievement') and the relative disposition of items about this axis (changes in the subordinate traits). The movements of a single item with respect to all the others over time may be difficult to interpret, but if we find consistent changes over time among items on, for example, *co-ordinate geometry*, or involving *decimal fractions*, or *long division*, or *number bases other than ten*, with respect to other items, then we may infer that mathematics itself as taught in schools is changing. This methodology provides the means not merely of detecting this change but of measuring it. The APU have the first real opportunity of doing this.

Conclusion

It is time to end the debate on such questions as 'Can item banking work?', despite a peculiarly British predilection for such discussion. We have been arguing for decades about whether or not comprehensive schools can work although in many countries both more and less developed than Britain, comprehensive schools have been the norm for a very long time. Britain is the home of the Flat Earth Society, and there is probably a sect somewhere that holds to the belief that the giraffe is impossible. Despite the initial work on item banking carried out in Britain in the late 1960s we still have very little to show in terms of operational experience. Item banks however are in every-day use in the United States (particularly on the West Coast) and in Australia (particularly New South Wales, Victoria and Tasmania). They are under active develop-ment in several EEC countries, in Canada, India, Israel, Indonesia and Malaysia. No doubt testing agencies in other countries are also involved, but the news has not yet got back to us.

Item banks cannot provide any final answer to the problems of educational assessment and measurement. As far as I know, nobody has ever claimed that they could. They do, however, represent a giant step forward from standardized tests. Those that have been frustrated by the limitations inherent in standardized testing have good reason for optimism about the future. Item banks are going to be useful to many; the issue now is how to make them work better.

References

Choppin, B. H. (1978a) *Item Banking and the Monitoring of Achievement*. Research in Progress Series No. 1. Slough: NFER.

—— (1978b) The national monitoring of academic standards. Paper read to the National Council on Measurement in Education, Toronto.

—— (1978c) *Psychometric Developments Relating to Item Banking: A Select Annotated Bibliography*. Slough: NFER.

Dobby, J. & Duckworth, D. (1979) *Objective Assessment by Means of Item Banking*. Schools Council Examinations Bulletin No. 40. London: Evans/Methuen Educational.

DuBois, P. H. (1968) A test-dominated society: China 1115BC–1905AD'. *Proceedings of the 1964 Invitational Conference on Testing Problems*. Princeton, NJ: Educational Testing Service.

Engel, I. (1976) The differential effect of three different mathematics curricula on student's achievement through the use of sample-free scaling. MA thesis, Tel Aviv University.

Goldstein, H. (1979) Consequences of using the Rasch model for educational assessment. *Brit. Educ. Research Journal* **5**, 211–20.

—— & Blinkhorn, S. (1977) Monitoring educational standards – an inappropriate model. *Bulletin of the Brit. Psych. Soc.* **30**, 309–11.

Greenbaum, W., Garet, M. S. & Solomon, E. R. (1977) *Measuring Educational Progress: A Study of the National Assessment.* New York: McGraw-Hill.

Lord, F. M. (1952) A theory of test scores. *Psychometrica Monograph*, 1–84.

—— (1977) Practical applications of item characteristic curve theory. *J. Educ. Meas.* **14** (7), 117–38.

Mead, R. (1976) The assessment of fit of data to the Rasch model through analysis of residuals. Unpublished doctoral thesis, University of Chicago.

Ping-Ti Ho, (1962) *The Ladder of Success in Imperial China.* New York: Columbia University Press.

Rasch, G. (1960) *Probabilistic Models for Some Intelligence and Attainment Tests.* Copenhagen: Teknisk Forlag.

Scriven, M. (1976) The methodology of evaluation. *Perspectives of Curriculum Evaluation: AERA Monograph Series on Curriculum Evaluation*, 1. Chicago: Rand McNally.

Shoemaker, D. M. (1975) Toward a framework for achievement testing. *Rev. Educ. Res.* **45**, 127–47.

Wood, R. (1978) Fitting the Rasch Model – a heady tale. *Br. J. Math. Statist. Psychol.* **31**, 27–32.

Wood, R. & Skurnik, L. S. (1969) *Item Banking.* Slough: NFER.

Wright, B. D. (1977) Solving measurement problems with the Rasch model. *J. Educ. Meas.* **14**, 97–116.

Conclusion

Colin Lacey and Denis Lawton

The idea of accountability

Clearly there is a need for a policy on evaluation and accountability. Teachers and pupils need to have systematic feedback about successes and failures connected with teaching programmes, whether these are traditional programmes or the result of new curriculum development projects. Similarly, there must be a place for accountability in any public educational system – the real question is 'what kind of accountability?' Accountability is in itself neither good nor bad; it all depends on the kind of accountability employed or perhaps the appropriateness of the model of accountability being used. It would be arrogance of an extreme kind for teachers to claim unrestricted autonomy over the control of the curriculum and, also, to deny the need to 'account for' resources placed at their disposal, or children placed in their care. If teachers are responsible, then it is reasonable to expect them to 'report back' on their responsibilities (not simply to account to themselves). The first essential question is 'to whom should they be responsible?' The second is 'what form should this accountability take?'

Hugh Sockett (1980) has illustrated the difficulty of answering the question 'accountability to whom?' by listing the various possible answers (or combinations of answers):

(a) To individual pupils and parents;
(b) Pupils and their parents as part of the community;
(c) The teachers' employers, e.g. LEA;
(d) The providers of the resources, both LEA and government;
(e) Professional peers inside and outside the school;
(f) Other relevant educational institutions, e.g. universities.
(g) The public;
(h) Industry including the trade unions.

. . . manifestly such a list is far too slack and diffuse for us to be able to build a system of accountability from it . . . (Sockett, 1980, p. 14).

Similar difficulties exist regarding the accountability which is appropriate for teachers. Is the teacher accountable to the public for producing good citizens? If so, what is a good citizen? Is a teacher accountable to employers for school leavers' inability to cope with obsolete tests or their unwillingness to submit to antiquated views on discipline?

The problem of accountability and evaluation is extremely complex. Nevertheless, a danger exists that in the midst of this complexity, simple solutions will be suggested or even imposed. In its starkest form such a 'solution' would be to reduce evaluation to a simple testing programme across a narrow range of objectives, and to equate accountability with telling teachers what they ought to be doing – often as part of a general 'back to basics' campaign.

Lessinger (1972) adds another dimension to the problem: 'accountability suggests penalties and rewards; accountability without redress or incentive is mere rhetoric' (p. 29).

If this is the case, then teachers must make sure that any system of accountability that is adopted is one which is appropriate to educational processes, not to a version of crude input-output model. Accountability as a concept came to education via business and government: before taking on any model that is packaged with the concept, the appropriateness of the model should be carefully examined from theoretical and practical points of view.

The 'behavioural objectives' approach

The American experience in this respect is extremely interesting and relevant, illustrating the point made above about the business origins of the accountability metaphor. Myron Atkin (1979) has suggested that when Lyndon Johnson became President of the USA he was so impressed with Robert McNamara's success in applying the managerial techniques of The Ford Motor Company to the Department of Defense that he required all government departments to adopt procedures such as management by objectives, cost-benefit analysis, systems analysis and planned programme budgeting. One reason for Johnson's enthusiasm was that it enabled non-specialists to control the professional military men:

> it was easier to deal with admirals advocating the construction of new battleships competing with generals pressing for new bombers, if objective seeming procedures could be employed to help the non-specialist President make the final decision. How much explosive could be delivered reliably and at what cost by air and by ship? which was more dependable? how much 'bang for the buck'? The procedure looked effective, tidy and fair – and it resulted in diminution of the power of the professional specialist and an increase in that of the politician and, ultimately, the civil servant. (Atkin, 1979)

Seminars were held in 1965, 1966 and 1967, to encourage

administrators in departments such as Health, Education, and Welfare to learn from the Department of Defense. Input and output began to be applied to the schools and welfare programmes. The 'behavioural objectives' view of curriculum planning already existed, of course, in education. In 1949 Ralph Tyler had published his influential book *Basic Principles of Curriculum and Instruction*, and in 1956 Bloom and his colleagues had produced *The Taxonomy of Educational Objectives*. The background in theory, therefore, already existed; the 1960s and 1970s translated bad theory into bad practice. It is just possible that without the justification of this behavioural objectives model, the new approach to educational planning by objectives would have met with greater opposition and more effective resistance. Behavioural objectives became a major tool in the early American accountability projects because of their apparent precision. Vague aims like 'fostering good citizenship' became unacceptable and teachers were required to introduce a greater degree of clarity and precision into their planning.

> Some voices were heard suggesting that schools should strive for goals that went beyond those that could be stated readily in behavioural terms, and that behavioural objectives were undesirably limiting. However, the apparent logic of behaviourally stated objectives had tremendous appeal, not only to the general public when it heard about them, but to many teachers and school administrators. (Atkin, 1979, p. 6)

Some of the attempts to apply the management by objectives approach to education in the USA will be described below.

Performance contracting

This became extremely popular in the late 1960s and early 1970s. In some school districts a contract was drawn up between schools and private organizations whereby the outside organization was commissioned to work with teachers to raise the achievement levels of the children in that school. The fee paid to the firm depended on the time it took to reach specified levels of attainment, and the levels that were ultimately reached. Many of these schemes were supported by federal government.

Opposition to performance contracting came first from testing experts who complained that the tests being used were simply not suitable (they were norm-referenced rather than criterion-referenced); these kinds of objections tended to be ignored. Performance contracting was almost a complete failure. Evidence appeared indicating fraud by some contractors – teachers were given the tests in advance in order to enable them to 'teach to the tests'. This is a good example of the failure of that kind of management approach.

The Michigan State accountability system

This was one of the best-known examples of accountability and evaluation. It had six main features:

1   common goals are defined;
2   common goals are translated into objectives;
3   school needs are assessed to meet the objectives;
4   'alternative delivery systems' are tested;
5   a local evaluation capability for measurement and assessment is developed;
6   feedback from the results guides the state and local practices.

In this system the teacher is accountable to the public or taxpayer. Educational administrators become 'accountants' or 'auditors'. The teacher is not accountable to pupils or parents or professional colleagues. Pupils' performance is assessed against pre-specified objectives measured by standardized tests. Publicity is given to the test results and improved test scores may result in bonus payment for teachers, or increased grants for schools.

The disadvantages of this system are similar to the nineteenth-century 'payment by results' system in England. The assumption is made that measuring a child's performance is a fair way of evaluating a teacher's skill or hard work. As every teacher knows, there are many other factors involved. Above all, such test programmes encourage a narrowing of the curriculum and a style of teaching which is over-didactic. Teachers concentrate not on what they believe to be most worthwhile, but on those items which they think will 'come up' in a test. There are also considerable administrative burdens placed on teachers in administering and checking the tests, thus giving them less time to do worthwhile teaching. There are, of course, many other theoretical objections to the Michigan type of programme which will be examined later in this section.

NAEP

Both of the above must be clearly distinguished from the National Assessment of Educational Progress (NAEP). NAEP is part of the work of the Education Commission of the States (ECS) which is a non-profit-making organization formed by inter-state arrangements in 1966 to encourage relationship between governors, state legislators and educationists at all level. Forty-six states, Puerto Rico and the Virgin Islands are also members of ECS. (NAEP is located within the ECS headquarters in Denver, Colorado. It has a staff of more than seventy and its budget uses up more than 40 per cent of ECS total funds. Most of the NAEP budget is paid for out of federal funds.) Like the APU, NAEP is interested in measuring not individual pupils but groups, assessing how they perform in relation to a given objective. This is so that specific problems may be isolated by means of this 'single item reporting'. For example, one famous item illustrated that in July 1975, only 1 per cent of

American seventeen-year-old students could balance a cheque book.

Another purpose of national assessment is to record changes in achievement over time. Ten learning areas have been studied:

1 reading;
2 writing;
3 citizenship;
4 social studies;
5 science;
6 mathematics;
7 music;
8 literature;
9 art;
10 career and occupational development.

The objectives within each area were agreed upon by teachers, administrators and lay persons. Exercise packages to measure progress on those objectives were designed and administered. Approximately 100,000 individuals have been involved in the testing programme in four age groups: nine, thirteen, seventeen, and twenty-six to thirty-five.

Most of the exercises designed for testing are multichoice items. Some are, however, individually administered by means of an interview (e.g. when a student is asked to sight-read a line of music, or perform a laboratory experiment in science). All tests are administered by trained researchers not teachers. Group results are made available according to sex, race, geographical region, parents' education, community size and age.

The programme, which began in 1969, has many resemblances with the Assessment of Performance Unit. Although a number of criticisms have been made about the programme, it is generally regarded with much greater favour by teachers and educationists than other accountability systems in the USA.

The Swedish experience with 'behavioural objectives'

In the experimental programmes preceding the Swedish comprehensive school reforms, the problem of ability grouping and other kinds of grouping was investigated. When social background and ability were held constant, ability grouping and class size were found to have little effect on achievement as measured by standardized tests. In other words, there was no real difference in measured performance between children in ability groups or in mixed ability groups. This was a much quoted and interesting example of a Swedish attempt to introduce evaluation as a way of accounting to the public before a change was made in the administrative structure of schools.

At a later date, however, an extensive re-analysis of the data took place which looked at other factors as well as the test results quoted above. This included instructional methods, curriculum content and teaching time. It was found that the tests used had only covered the most elementary part of the curriculum; their general content validity was low and the tests were not equally fair to all the classes being compared. Above all, it became clear that behind the apparent equal scoring on the tests there were considerable differences in the number of lessons needed in order to achieve mastery in the basic skills measured.

Dahloff (1979) summarizes the Swedish experience as follows:

(a) That conventional standardized achievement tests have inherent risks as instruments of evaluation for accountability since they seldom cover more than the common core or very basic curriculum units. Thus, as the sole instrument, they may be highly deceptive because of lacking content validity.

(b) That test scores may be the outcomes of very different educational processes with regard to teaching methods, contents and time, but also with respect to the restrictions exerted by various environmental and administrative frame factors under which the teachers have to do their jobs with a certain group of students, who have given initial characteristics. Thus, the teaching task may have varying difficulty from the point of view of the school and teacher, due to the student group as well as to environmental obstacles.

(c)   That test scores as such have a low information value about the outlying processes as well as the environmental and administrative frame conditions, necessary to understand and appreciate the skills and efforts needed to fulfil a certain educational goal, while information about the students initial ability, frame conditions and the main characteristics of the teaching process permits a fairly accurate prediction of the outcomes.

(d)   Consequently, there is a strong need to redirect and supplement evaluation strategies with information about the environmental conditions as well as about the teaching processes. (Dahloff, 1979, p. 61)

Criticism of the 'behavioural objectives' model

Underlying the criticisms made about the US and Swedish evaluation experience is a theoretical objection to the behavioural objectives model, and the kind of accountability which simply demands 'results' in terms of higher test scores.

The objections to the behavioural objectives model are both theoretical and practical, but only the theoretical problem will be discussed in this section. The behavioural objectives approach rests on the assumption that for all teaching and learning situations it is possible and desirable to specify in advance the precise changes which will be observed (and measured) in pupil behaviour. The essence of a behavioural objective is that it must be a pre-specified change in pupil behaviour which is testable and measurable. One major objection to this is that in some kinds of learning situations it is neither possible nor desirable to predict pupil responses: in an English literature lesson, for example, the teacher must have ideas about the *kind* of response which he hopes for as well as those he would find disappointing, but these are not precise changes in behaviour – each individual's response to a work of art is unique. Similarly, in a history lesson, there is often no one right answer to a question – a pupil's response has to be rated according to several different criteria such as knowledge of the evidence, ability to evaluate the evidence and draw conclusions from it, ability to argue logically, etc. These may be regarded as general objectives, but they certainly do not qualify as precise behavioural objectives. Many would argue, however, that without such practices education would be greatly impoverished.

A second fundamental objection to the behavioural objectives model concerns the nature of behaviour. Many philosophers have criticized behaviourist psychologists in general for limiting the notion of behaviour to what can be perceived and measured by psychological observers; others have applied this general criticism to the behavioural objectives model in education or planning. To return to our example about a poetry lesson, we can see that when presented with a new poem a pupil may undergo many different kinds of mental experience of an educationally desirable kind without emitting any kind of observable behavioural changes: he may be profoundly moved or excited and stimulated to read more poetry, or perhaps to write his own, but the behaviourist psychologist and the behavioural objectives curriculum expert would only be interested in what they could observe and measure. This is to distort and trivialize both the nature of human activities and the process of education. Some kinds of educational experience are better judged by the quality of input rather than the measured output in terms of changes in behaviour, but that view is totally denied by behavioural objectives curriculum theory.

We have already seen that one of the dangers of the APU is that it could be associated with a model of curriculum planning by behavioural objectives. The curriculum would then become narrow and rigid, teachers would teach to the test, and the content of the curriculum would tend to become trivialized.

Even if this could be avoided by the APU programme, there remains the greater problem of LEA testing procedures. It is by now clear that LEAs will be encouraged to use some APU materials to develop their own tests (probably in conjunction with NFER). These tests will not be subject to the constraints imposed upon the APU – for example, it will be possible to identify schools or even classes and individual children. The pressure on teachers to produce higher test scores will then be very great indeed. Many LEAs are already developing tests along these lines. This narrow view of evaluation combined with an accountability model which will demand the release of such information to the public could be extremely damaging.

Alternative models of accountability

In view of the deficiencies of the behavioural objectives approach, it seems necessary to look for alternative models of accountability and evaluation. We have seen that the accountability concept or metaphor is more closely connected with business than with education. If it is to be applied to education (and possibly to other government institutions) then the metaphor needs to be considerably modified. Most of the discussion so far has been concerned with one-way 'upward' accountability, that is, a subordinate giving an account to a superior for money spent, resources used, etc. But democratic accountability should be a two-way process: the teacher is accountable to pupils as well as to the headteacher or the inspector, and the headteacher is accountable to his assistant teachers as well as to governors or the LEA. This view of accountability is close to the idea of 'open government' expressed in the OECD Report of the DES and the Tenth Report of the Expenditure Committee of the House of Commons, both of which complained about the level of secrecy which has constantly been maintained within the DES (so much so, that the Parliamentary Committee was denied access to a good deal of the information they wanted).

Michael Eraut (1979) developed this idea when he conceives of accountability in terms of *information*. His alternative to a more centralized system of education based on central accountability, with teachers as closely controlled employees, is a concept of delegation with teachers as autonomous accountable professionals. Eraut develops the kind of information-giving processes which would be needed at school level in a system of accountable professional teachers.

The idea of accountability as information giving has a good deal in common with Barry MacDonald's work on evaluation. MacDonald sees evaluation in terms of 'briefing decision makers' and suggests three possible models of evaluation: bureaucratic, autocratic and democratic. For MacDonald, democratic evaluation attempts to be an information service to the whole community. Sponsorship by one group such as the bureaucrats does not give a special claim to advice or secret information. The assumption behind democratic evaluation is 'value pluralism', i.e. that there is no consensus about basic values and basic educational issues. The only value which can be assumed is the desirability of an informed citizenry. The role of the evaluator is thus that of an honest broker.

Another alternative model is that of school self-evaluation. Tony Becher (1979) suggests that schools can no longer be labelled simply as good or bad, but should be judged as good or bad examples of the kind of schools they wish to be. Such a view would mean making public (or at least semi-public) not only test results or examination successes but the criteria by which the school would wish to be judged. Arrangements would then be necessary for some kind of 'peer group review' to decide how successful a school was within its own terms of reference. This is perhaps more 'relativist' than many of us would accept, and it would also represent a much more autonomous policy for schools than operates, for example, at higher education level through the CNAA.

John Elliott has also written a number of papers about 'Self-accounting Schools' (1979, 1980) and is currently directing a research project (the Cambridge Accountability project) exploring with a few secondary schools the problems they face in trying to develop their own accountability procedures. Elliott feels that schools might be allowed to write their own accounts or reports which would then be checked by external auditors prior to release for publication. But not all accountability problems are solved by such proposals – inevitably we have to deal with wider political issues and questions of minimum standards and the content of core curricula.

What is clear, however, is that no school should be judged simply on a crude set of test results or examination grades. Test results can be presented in much more sophisticated ways and still be meaningful to the public (Gray, 1979), but, even so, tests should only form part of an evaluation and accountability system rather than be seen as the whole picture.

General summing–up

Richard Pring in his paper was concerned with the philosophical problems of the APU theoretical model – in particular, the concept of development. Harvey Goldstein was equally concerned about the appropriateness of item banking in a testing programme of this kind. But there is an even more fundamental semi-political question to be asked: even if it were given (and it is not) that the APU approach is the right one as a model for studying or investigating a particular educational system, does it necessarily follow that the model could or should be used as an administrative device for *controlling* certain aspects of that system? Graham Tall's paper cast a good deal of doubt on the practical aspects of APU testing and the influence that such testing programmes are almost inevitably going to have on the content of the curriculum and the teaching styles used by teachers. A major problem here is that while the APU testing programme is looked upon as an academic exercise or experiment, then the APU testers and researchers are responsible to an academic community. However, if the APU becomes a national system of establishing or monitoring standards, and even more if the APU testing programme legitimizes LEA blanket testing, then those involved in the testing are no longer accountable to an academic community but to administrators and indirectly to the public at large. Then the testing programme begins to be seen as a method of producing a crude system of league tables whereby schools are judged by test results (irrespective of catchment areas), and such evidence is even used as a basis for closing schools or for criticizing teachers and headteachers.

Bruce Choppin makes a good case in his paper for the merits of the 'Danish system' as compared with the 'Chinese model', but a number of important practical and political questions remain unanswered. Researchers cannot abdicate from their responsibilities by stating that their intentions in devising or administering tests were quite different from the uses to which the tests were ultimately put. It is here that we have to look very carefully at the American evidence. This is not altogether reassuring, although it might be said that the NAEP experience would suggest that we ought not to fear the APU as much as the unintended consequences of the APU in the form of LEA testing programmes. But even so, we ought not to exaggerate the value of NAEP or APU tests.

Harvey Goldstein's paper hints at the danger that a good

deal of money will be spent on tests which have very little educational feedback, although they may be very useful for local or national politicians. Tests of the NAEP or APU kind do not necessarily improve the quality of teaching or learning. Diagnostic tests would be much more productive in that way, but perhaps even more productive would be in-service programmes of education or professional development for teachers which would enable them to improve their own and their pupils' performance without elaborate testing machinery. For some readers that will be the important message in the first part of this book.

The main conclusions for researchers in the field can now be summarized. It is important that the theory and research methods used in evaluation and accountability exercises be rigorously examined. Clearly internal criticism is important, but Carl Parsons reminds us of the importance of maintaining a broadly based link with social science disciplines. Even if the reader disagrees with the idea of abandoning the term 'evaluation' the main point remains that these disciplines are often the origin of 'new' ideas in evaluation. This link remains crucial in another sense to evaluators and researchers in accountability who are subject to increasing pressures as they move closer to administrators, teachers and local and national politicians. The academic community with its injunction to 'increase our understanding' can act as an important counterweight to the pressures from politicians and administrators to manipulate or 'solve' things. We must remember that the definition of a problem is the greater part of deciding on the solution to the problem. It follows that the political pressures on researchers to define the problems in a way that delivers the right answers can be considerable. The research organization that stands out against these pressures risks having its research ignored and perhaps its future curtailed. The countervailing pressure from the research community might be slight but it is nevertheless important and its importance needs to be widely recog-

University of Sussex.

Gray, J. (1979) The statistics of accountability. *Education Policy Bulletin* 7.

Lessinger, L. M. (1972) Accountability for results: a basic challenge for America's schools. In L. M. Lessinger and R. W. Tyler (eds.) *Accountability in Education*. Washington, Ohio: Charles A. Jones.

MacDonald, B. (1978) Accountability, standards and the process of schooling. Mimeo, University of East Anglia.

Sockett, H. (ed.) (1980) *Accountability in the English Educational System*. London: Hodder & Stoughton.

Tyler, R. (1949) *Basic Principles of Curriculum and Instruction*. University of Chicago Press.

Index